The
Opposite
of
Loneliness

The
Opposite
of
Loneliness

What Does God Say?

By
REBECCA A. BALRAM

RESOURCE *Publications* · Eugene, Oregon

THE OPPOSITE OF LONELINESS
What Does God Say?

Resource Publications
An Imprint of Wipf and Stock Publishers
199 W. 8th Ave., Suite 3
Eugene, OR 97401

www.wipfandstock.com

PAPERBACK ISBN: 978-1-6667-4646-4
HARDCOVER ISBN: 978-1-6667-4647-1
EBOOK ISBN: 978-1-6667-4648-8

AUGUST 31, 2022 8:11 AM

Contents

Contents

Introduction

✳

Well guys, let's get moving!!! This book will take you an astounding 6 hours to read in total, but that's only if you're a slow reader—like myself but on the other hand, a much faster reader may take up half the time. Let's get one thing out of the way real quick, this book is not about singlehood—it's about loneliness. Many people mistake singlehood as loneliness, that's kind of not what I'm basing loneliness as since, you can be lonely even if your married or having thousands of followers and friends—that's just factual.

To be clear, I didn't write this book to "cure" your loneliness; loneliness may strike at any time and affect anyone. This book was written to help you take control and conquer your loneliness. I talked about my most personal observations and experiences—not to humiliate myself, but to show you that even I, as a PK, have similar troubles, very much like you, and you are not alone in your loneliness. This is how millions of other people feel on a daily. You are not the only one who feels this way, and you are not ungrateful or a disappointment because you do. In your defense, you're still young, and we all have more to discover and encounter with God.

My point is as you read on into this book, I guarantee that you'll find a much brighter and deeper outlook on your loneliness. Yes, loneliness is just a feeling, but it can stem and cause many other deadly factors in a young person' s life. This book discusses so many core topics for young Christian adults and teens that it's about to break a lot of silence. It describes how loneliness can be a starter for things like: depression, anxiety, body image issues, sexual temptation and many other things. Various discussions on characters from the bible who has experienced loneliness, especially Jesus who was the loneliest yet most famous guy to ever exist. It answers questions like, "Where or when does loneliness *attack* us the most?" This book is even filled with real-life relatable stories and testimonies. It speaks subtly on the demon of loneliness and what it can do to young adults. Reasoning topics like church hurt and loneliness in ministry, since a lot of young people—like myself, take up ministry at a young age. How to embrace loneliness as well as using your seclusion for the greater good—benefiting the Gospel of Jesus Christ. And lastly, answering the burning question of *"what is the opposite of loneliness?"*

Although, besides those things I totally get it, we grew up in an era of technology. We've seen so many non-Christians express themselves in relationships . . . at a very young age. We've seen them openly displaying their sin and worldly lives without judgement. They have hundreds of friends, thousands of followers and the world feeding them attention and fame. Then later, we ratio and compare ourselves too them, and we realize how lonely this Christian walk can be compared to the world. In my eyes, that's really sad and it needs to be addressed because we weren't supposed to be like them in the first place. We're called to be different, extra-ordinary and a royal priesthood. You are in this world, not of this world!

CHAPTER 1

What is Loneliness?

Is there really something called loneliness?

✳

My life seems so godforsaken.

I know what you may be thinking, that was very blunt but for me, sometimes bluntness is a good thing. Why? Because it reveals a truth and exposes a lie. Being who I am behind the mask of "Christian girl" or "Pastor's kid" has made people believe that I am seemingly perfect and content. Let me expose something to you, Christian or not, everyone feels discontentment. There's a lie the devil sets for individuals who think loneliness and discontentment is something they struggle with alone. Let's be real, all Satan does is lie. Let's begin to fight back and this book is a stepping stone for that.

"Why does it seem that everyone doesn't want to be friends with me, mom?" the tiny seven-year-old me asked. "Why is everyone so mean to me, it's only when my friends need money, homework or food, that's when they're nice to me." My mom looked at me with confusion. "If they only want your stuff, then they are not your friends. Friends are supposed to be nice to you regardless of what you have and don't have" she replied lovingly. *"God will send you the right people into your life."*

I suppose the most proper definition of the word loneliness that I can sum up is described as, "A negative emotional reaction to perceived alienation. Loneliness is sometimes referred to as social pain, which is a psychological mechanism that drives people to seek social interactions and interpersonal relationships. It is frequently linked to an undesirable lack of engagement and intimacy or openness."

For a long time in my life, it felt lonely. Hi, my name's Rebecca and I am an eighteen-year-old, new undergrad at University. I study Criminology and Criminal Justice and I do a minor in Speech Language Pathology and Audiology, I know—weird combo and long story. But for a long time, I have been begging God for some Godly company, some good friends or at least a good friend. I know many of you reading this book, somehow or the other feel as lonely as a selfie post on Instagram without any likes or as dry as a phone without any messages or interaction.

Loneliness is just another burdening emotion that we may all experience in our Christian life. Yes, we realize that God is always present with us since it is part of His character to be omnipresent. He never leaves us, but it doesn't mean we don't experience loneliness in the normal sense. There is a distinction to be made between being alone and being lonely. Being alone is the absence of company, whereas loneliness is unhappiness caused by the absence of companionship. Loneliness is an emotion that is all too familiar to me. Though, I may say that I have learnt to be content with God's presence, I would be dishonest if I said that loneliness somehow doesn't occasionally try to infiltrate my heart. It does, and probably every day of my life, if I permit it too.

Coming from my heart and how I have experienced it, I believe the perfect definition for being lonely would be, "Sitting at the lunch table all alone. The feeling of being lost without direction and help. It is a longing desire to be intimate and that does not necessarily mean romantically but to make friends and finally just laugh and have fun. To encounter an environment where it isn't toxic for once, just healthy conversation. And eventually, a Godly yet healthy and romantic relationship with someone that

God has desired me to be with, a divine connection." Miserably, it may seem like none of that is happening, is it? It's just you—and it's always just been you.

To make matters worse, I have no siblings. So, it's always just been me. Did I mention—I'm a pastor's kid, you already know— I'm literally even lonelier. Not a lot of people understand what it actually means to be a Pastor's kid and a lot of people avoid being friends with them too. That's okay though, because this book will take you on a journey of how I experienced loneliness and what God says to you amazing young people who also relate to that feeling of being lonely in this world.

At the beginning, there was a deep conversation between me and my mum. When I was younger, I first attended a non-Christian Primary School and made no friends. All the people there did not like or appreciate my presence to say the least. Unless these groups of bullies wanted money or food or a chance to really make fun of me, that was the only reason to really pay attention or act like they liked me. Those girls were so ruthless for no reason as well, there was absolutely no reason to dislike me. My parents made sure I had everything, I was clean and I was kind, I understood the principles of sharing and loving like Jesus loved even at that tender age. They just hated me—they'd say mean and ungodly words to me like, "just get rid of yourself, you ugly freakshow, your dumb or stop being so disgusting all the time."

Let me just really begin by saying, yes, I was hurt and I came home upset and sad every single day. Nonetheless, God adored me, I just didn't notice it, yet. I had yet to learn the worth I had in Christ. I think most of us are like that, we don't notice the in-depth love God really has for us and it's because God chose us, He called you blameless, beautiful inside and out. He is so fond of you, even from the minute you were conceived by your parents.

> Jer 1:5 Before I formed you in the womb I knew you, before you were born, I set you apart; I appointed you as a prophet to the nations.

> Ps 139:13–14 For you created my inner being; you knit me together in my mother's womb. 14 I praise you

because I am fearfully and wonderfully made; your works are wonderful; I know that fully well.

I know, these verses are quite well known—but if you don't know them it's honestly never too late to be familiar with them. God really said that regardless of how you look like to other people, regardless of what they say or think or do to you—no matter who you are and what you have, *beloved, I still love you.* Well, isn't that spectacularly awesome? To be loved by God Himself? A God who is so perfect, He looked at you who is flawed and a mess sometimes and said to you directly *"I love you, my child"* Amazing!

Many of you reading this book, have that feeling of being overlooked. You have that feeling of being unnoticed. Sometimes you feel so alienated from this world. It's almost like you don't even exist in this world—it's like there is no connection to your family, friends or even reality. So much that you're so lost about your future as well—*life just couldn't get worse.* God is saying to you that He genuinely cares about the fact you're lonely and sometimes feel lost in this world. His word says in:

> Isa 43:2 When you pass through the waters, I will be with you; and when you pass through the rivers, they will not sweep over you. When you walk through the fire, you will not be burned; the flames will not set you ablaze.

It may sound very *cliche* at the moment but listen to me when I say, "If God is all you have, then He is all you need." And for the past eighteen years and counting, I would definitely say that this statement is beyond the word true. That sentence holds so much power to it because of the fact that when you have God, who already knows and is everything, what is there exactly to need?

I believe that this generation specifically is jam-packed with the loneliest people. I don't think you guys realized that when God said this narrow road to heaven is lonely—He really means that it's lonely. We see every single day that teenagers are committing suicide because of reasons like being lonely—and there is no one around them to support and understand these days. Let's face the facts, everyone is focused on their own life and that's totally normal. It may feel like no one has your back but here it is God is saying son or daughter, please understand that I know how you feel and don't let go of Me neither take your eyes off of Me.

> Jer 29:11 For I know the plans I have for you," declares the Lord, "plans to prosper you and not to harm you, plans to give you hope and a future.

> John 3:16 For God so loved the world that he gave his one and only Son, that whoever believes in him shall not perish but have eternal life.

You may be asking, "God, why do you love me?" well . . . He just does, He created you from the womb and He knew you from the very beginning. He knew that you were resilient enough to hang in there and regardless of what you do He's always going to love you. So much so, He has created an entire future and a whole love story between you and Him. I want you to remember the story between Peter and Jesus. I want you to consider the fact that Peter never asked Jesus if He loved him. Peter Knew He did. Instead, Jesus asked Peter . . . three times. Peter never had to ask that question; he was well aware how fond Jesus was of him.

> John 21:15–17 When they had finished eating, Jesus said to Simon Peter, "Simon son of John, do you love me more than these?" "Yes, Lord," he said, "you know that I love you." Jesus said, "Feed my lambs." 16 Again Jesus said, "Simon son of John, do you love me?" He answered, "Yes, Lord, you know that I love you." Jesus said, "Take care of my sheep." 17 The third time he said to him, "Simon son of John, do you love me?" Peter was hurt because Jesus asked him the third time, "Do you love me?" He said, "Lord, you know all things; you know that I love you." Jesus said, "Feed my sheep.

CHAPTER 2

The Battles of Loneliness in the Bible

Did anyone from the Bible suffer with loneliness?

✳

G od loves to use messed up men and women." Hence the reason the Bible has so many exciting but devastating stories about men and women who battled loneliness. I know what you're thinking, the Bible is not as exciting as I am describing it. You're a little right, sometimes it really isn't but, some of the stories are really interesting, for example, the story between Jacob, Leah and Rachel, lots of excitement there, I'm not going to lie. Moses leading an entire generation out of slavery. Noah and this gigantic ark that's way more stable than the Titanic. The bravest Queen Esther who saved her country. Elijah, who conquers the day and faces Jezebel. The woman by the well. Saul who became Paul, God was the one who changed his name and he was a cruel crusader who threw Christians in imprisonment, destroyed chapels and churches, and even oversaw their executions in order to halt the spread of Christianity. He was so devoted to his Jewish beliefs that he wished to exterminate all Believers and God turned his whole life around. I can think of so many more stories from the Bible that are considerably more thrilling than you may imagine, and guess what? God performed something supernatural in each one. Totally rad.

My point is though that if you ever stop to think that you're lonely because you're so messed up and you make mistakes. Think again because God is definitely planning to use you. These men and women I listed out above who carried out God's purpose, *were far from perfect.* Take it from me, I have made some questionable and ridiculous mistakes, but God has used me so much that I literally expose myself in front of crowds now and that may sound embarrassing but God literally uses your mistakes to inspire and amaze people of the things He has done for you. You're not lonely because you're messed up, you're admitted to be lonely because *God wants you for Himself.* This is just one of the many strategies God uses to teach and mold you into His masterpiece. That's how much value you hold to God. You were created especially for this lonely period in your life. God only does this to protect you, not harm you and that may be how the devil wants you to see it. As you read on you will have a better idea of what I'm saying and the points I'm trying to draw. If you have reached thus far in this book, the journey has only just begun.

In this chapter, there will be explanations on different stories in the Bible with people who have been through this battle called loneliness. But before I do, I would just like to remind you guys that it is never too late with God, no matter how you feel and no matter where your mental health lies. *He is still fond of you.* What I think you should know is, your sin and your problems aren't too big or messed up for God. He sees and knows everything about you, inside and out.

A JEALOUS WIFE (GENESIS 29)

In the book of Genesis Chapter 29, it talks about the story between Jacob, Rachel and Leah. Jacob's first wife was Leah. The second wife was her sister, Rachel. Leah was always convinced that her sister was more loved than she was, and she was correct. Can you imagine fighting for your husband's love and affection with your sister?

Leah was described as having weary eyes which in my opinion would have been so beautiful. Her sister on the other hand was sort of her competition because her physical appearance and body shape was much more appealing to Jacob. Do you ever feel not handsome enough? Not pretty enough? Like you're just average? You're really just not that amazing so your appearance is always overlooked? God is saying you don't have to be Rachel. Just be you. I created you the way you are and have said in my word that you have no flaws.

> Song 4:7 You are altogether beautiful, my darling; there is no flaw in you.

In the book Songs of Solomon, Solomon was the one who said this verse to his dark beautiful lover. In the book she was identified as insecure and afraid for Solomon to see her body. She was black and to her, she wasn't beautiful. She felt very ugly and therefore, could not understand why Solomon wanted her. The purpose for the book called Song of Solomon was to construct the love between Christ and the human soul. You see God doesn't exactly care about your outside appearance, He better appreciates your heart, although He did create every single person in His likeness. Therefore, He is aware of your beauty.

The point I am getting at is that God loves you a lot deeper than a normal human would. It depicts that this world will compare and contrast your body and flaws. This world will pick you apart and analyze whether you are lovable or if you deserve to be lonely forever. God is saying that whatever the world tells you about yourself, *it is a lie.* He knows that one day your loneliness will change. The world may say otherwise but you can trust when He says something.

A MOTHER AND SON SENT TO DEATH (GENESIS 21)

Hagar was Sarah's servant who bore Abraham a son, Ishmael. Sarah's envy of Hagar leads to the expulsion of Hagar and her son into the desert of Beersheba. She even sat down to die because she and her son were completely abandoned, helpless and unable to seek assistance. Can you imagine how lonely she was for herself and her child?

Reading this story made me think about how single parents feel, especially those parents who are barely thriving out there, in the world, with minimum wage jobs. People who were abandoned by their families for having insecurities and mental challenges. Teenage girls or women who were abandoned for being pregnant before marriage. Orphans who were left in the hospitals to die because their parents ran away. How lonely do these people probably feel? And it's the same concept with Hagar and Ishmael. God did pull through for Hagar and Ishmael when the angel showed up and then God provided Hagar with a well of water. But, at verse 20 of the story it read that:

> Gen 21:20 God was with the boy as he grew up. He lived in the desert and became an archer.

Notice that Ishmael, regardless of the situation, regardless of how lonely he and his mother felt and let's think of the fact that they had nothing in the wilderness, yet, *Ishmael found a purpose in his loneliness.* He became an archer. Not only that but Ishmael's future was pretty enticing, more than you would expect. *God promised Ishmael that He would raise up a great nation of his own.* And you better believe it, he did.

Fellow youngsters, the moral of this is that you can rest in God's promises when you feel the bondage of loneliness. *God doesn't lie*, we all know this. Yet, when we are caught up in our loneliness, we forget God and we ignore His promises over our life. Ponder on the fact that Ishmael did not use His background and his past as an excuse to run away from his purpose and dwell in his loneliness. A lot of us need to realize that God really desires better and far greater for us. Aim to be nothing like Hagar, especially the crying and giving up part but try harder to be like Ishmael who conquered His loneliness and proceeded to rightfully fulfill his purpose with God.

A BAD SISTER (NUMBERS 12)

Miriam was Moses' sister. She questioned Moses' leadership as a result of her jealousy. Her punishment was to be infected with leprosy and to be isolated outside of the camp for seven days. Despite Moses and Aaron's pleadings to God on her behalf, she had to remain outside the camp for seven days before being restored. Seven days does not seem like a long time until you consider how much risk she was in on her own. Loneliness left her defenseless and insecure.

How many of you have ever been sent to your room as punishment after you and your siblings were fighting? Many of us were sent away to our rooms as a punishment. Notice that whenever that happens you are left alone to think about whatever you did or what you may have been fighting about. Not just that, you're left with your own thoughts and when you're left, these vulnerable emotions start kicking in like: sadness, insecurity, anger, fear and pride. When you're left in those moments—*pray*. Get to know God. Yes, you're alone but you don't have to be lonely. God is with you at all times.

> Deut 31:6 Be strong and courageous. Do not be afraid or terrified because of them, for the Lord your God goes with you; he will never leave you nor forsake you.

When I say, "Get to know God" I really mean to form a relationship with Him. understand His humor, His ways, the way He speaks, understand His word and really just *rest in His presence* knowing that God is all you ever really need and He has everything under control.

I am one of those individuals that is extremely people-pleasing. As a result, I try to do my best at everything I do: academics, sports, writing, singing, even baking and cooking, something as trivial as speaking, I put my best foot forward because I am very conscious of people's opinion of me. I know, that's so unhealthy and it gets so frustrating because I do none of these things for fun or entirely for God. I feel like I just do it because of the fact that I am a pastor's kid and I have expectations and people are expecting nothing less than perfection. All I know is that it causes me so much pain and frustration, most times out of nowhere I sit down and cry. It gets really lonely on this end, but I have learned to *rest in God's amazing presence,* whenever or wherever I feel like this. Just feeling his anointing and knowing He's here with me brings me the most peace. Worship music as well calms me down. I do recommend but *talking to Jesus about everything is the best decision I have ever made.*

A FEARFUL PROPHET (1 KINGS 17)

Elijah was summoned to prophesy against Ahab, King of Israel, and to announce a famine sent by God. Of course, Elijah had to flee for his life shortly after. He went into the wilderness, where ravens provided him food. When the water ran out, God exiled him even more, all the way to Zarephath. He eventually found himself in the home of a widow and her son. Even though Elijah performed God's will, he remained an outcast far from his homeland.

Have you ever been bullied at school, your own family or where you work? Well listen, most of the time when that happens, someone's jealous of you. It's the same concept as Jezebel running after Elijah, just so she could kill him. When Elijah prayed and God set the fires from Heaven—everyone turned to the Almighty and she hated it. Elijah was horrified when he heard this. He believed that this miracle would inspire the people to rise up against Jezebel, but she stayed in power, and Ahab was unable to stop her.

Being bullied is one of the loneliest things someone can ever go through. I would know, I was bullied my entire primary school life and didn't have the slightest clue, why? One of the things my dad said to me is that demons can lurk in anyone, children or adults and it controls them. Demons know when they see a light, so they try to dim or put out the light that God has placed inside of you. The devil knows when he sees a God-fearing man or woman in the making, he will do literally anything to take that from you. He will try to steal your joy, steal your peace and steal your future. Don't let it shake your faith because *God has set you up for greatness*, and you have to do is keep trusting Him

A jezebel spirit can lurk inside anyone at any time. Sometimes, it's generational or even environmental, it depends. They get the behavior from their parents or school itself. As I said before, the school I went to wasn't Christian-based. I was even victimized by teachers because of my faith. They made fun of my parents too because they were pastors. For me it was the loneliest I have ever felt, I mean what would I know? I was so young. I would have spoken to God and asked Him, God, when will this ever stop? For some of you, it will be like that and it's really Satan wanting to discourage and manipulate you to stop being who you are in Christ. He's crazy jealous because of your identity and he's very aware of the greatness instilled inside of you.

Jezebel will enter your life at some point and they will come in to hurt you and try to manipulate your purpose, it can be through parents, teachers, friends, people you're dating and even in your own church. And don't even get me started, churches are lurking with such individuals and as a Pastors child, they target you first and your family.

Always remember guys, *to recognise* your loneliness. Most of the time it's the people around you that makes you feel lonely and discouraged. Surround yourself with the right company. If those demotivating people are from your family or relatives, I'm really sorry to hear that. Fortunately, Christianity is about leaving your birth family (not physically though) and joining a Godly Christian family (your church or youth ministry) There are mentors around you if you search carefully, God provides a support system such as your Pastor and his wife or even your youth leaders. Sometimes it's that aunt or uncle from church that you can latch on too for advice at any time, just make sure they're *trustworthy.*

A LONELY PROPHET (JEREMIAH)

God chose Jeremiah to be a prophet. His was indeed a lonely calling. Jeremiah, often known as the Weeping Prophet, was restricted from marrying and thus had no wife or children. Jeremiah was frequently shunned by those he was supposed to serve when he was summoned to preach words of repentance. When those you wish to serve and love, come to reject you, the agony is palpable and his loneliness came as a result of his commitment and obedience to God.

How many of us crave romantic love? But there's literally no one interested or no one that you're interested in. Dating is a very large topic; I might just create a separate book but in dating we tend to believe that God will somehow send our person to us. Which is sometimes true, I mean Adam was sleeping and then Eve came, right? Sometimes, it's as easy as that. Although, not many people are called to get married. Jeremiah was special in a sense that he wasn't called for that, his calling didn't consist of marriage or kids. I could just imagine how he felt and longed for someone to just love him and for him to have a partner for life to grow old with. He was sad and his sadness stemmed from his loneliness.

We perpetually say that God is a jealous God, and it's true, God wanted Jeremiah all to Himself. You see, when we worship material things or people, God tends to get 'jealous.' God is envious of His relationship with His people because He adores and cherishes them and does not want idolatry to corrupt them. After giving the instruction not to worship idols, God describes himself as a jealous God in the Ten Commandments. I would honestly be so honored if God told me He wanted me all to Himself, that's just so amazing, since I am imperfect after all. Think about it this way, it's the fact that God has taken you thus far, He wanted you and He called you to be all for Him. It is an honor in itself to be and do anything for God. That in itself should keep anyone going but the way you feel about it, whether it's the fear of being single or married, it totally is valid and understandable. With that being mentioned, it's also not ungrateful at all, if you feel such a way. Just know that with every desire you have, God planted it for a special reason. You may not understand right now, but trust God to write your story because He distinctly mentioned that He knows the plans He has set for us. Trusting God can be scary, it causes you to question but He promised that all good things happen to those that love God.

The question remains, *were you one of those kids who were always picked last?* Like you just weren't a favorite and it hurt you. I was one of those kids who was never really spoken too much or hardly noticed. I was kind of chubby and awkward. It never felt good knowing you weren't a favorite or weren't important, so much that you were shunned by many people. I feel you. But listen, *you are not walking on eggshells with God*, you can be all of you because His scripture says that He chose you first and He adores you no matter what you do. You don't have to be scared to upset Him or disappoint Him because He truly is fond of you, regardless. You are seen as blameless in His eyes.

> John 15:16 You did not choose me, but I chose you and appointed you so that you might go and bear fruit—fruit that will last—and so that whatever you ask in my name the Father will give you.

He chose you along with your loneliness, He chose you knowing you would be broken about traumatic and unhealed things in your life and He chose you realizing fully that you are imperfect and you may fail Him every day. Yet, He still chose to call you son and He chose to call you His daughter, both princes and princesses of His kingdom and that should be an honor to wake up too every day of your life.

LONELY KING DAVID

> Ps 142:4 Look and see, there is no one at my right hand; no one is concerned for me. I have no refuge; no one cares for my life.

David's ascension to the throne was rigorous and time-consuming. He spent time traveling in the wilderness to avoid King Saul. Did he still experience loneliness after ascending to the crown? You may be encircled by individuals who are only friendly to you because it benefits them. Even a King's wealth and power cannot compensate for genuine connection and belonging.

Let's self-examine ourselves right now. Ask yourself: are my friends, just friends with me because they love me and want the best for me or do they want something from me? Do they applaud my wins or do they give jealous glances?

I remember very recently that I was talking to this guy who friended me on Facebook and happened to message me on my Messenger. I know the Holy Spirit at the time was totally trying to tell me no, do not respond, and guess what . . . I did. And he proceeded to talk to me, never asking my name or anything like that. He came on very easily and the entire time I was being kind of rude, not going to lie, because I felt something so off about him. He asked me, "Can we get to know each other and eventually meet at the mall?" I was laughing so hard in my room because it's like we just met, why are you coming off so easily? Or where in your mind is it okay to do this so quickly?

Here's the funny part, he was non-Christian so I knew this already wasn't going to work from the start but what's actually hilarious is that I asked if he had an Instagram account and he told me *no*. Later that evening, I was scrolling on Instagram and his name just popped up in my recommendations, out of nowhere. Now, I know this isn't coincidental. Guys, he was literally a player and had ungodly pictures of girls on his profile. It may be just a little white lie, right? Boys will be boys, right? All I can say is thank you Lord for directing this situation because *I know that the man God is preparing for me wouldn't have lied*, especially in the first couple seconds. I know for a fact the real reason he wanted to meet me was for the purpose of hooking up. He was being nice to me and sweet-talked me the entire time because he wanted something from me, kind of like what the devil does, he makes his ideas of promising fame, power and money look spectacular but in reality, it's a trap.

In all honesty, *I absolutely despise hook-up culture*, but the moral of this is to be very discreet and cautious when picking your friends, even partners and the persons who you chose to speak and surround yourself with. There are sharks in the water waiting for prey and sometimes the devil creates doppelgangers of men and women to hinder the divine connection God has in stored for you.

The Bible literally talks about good and bad friends and I know many of us, including myself, our parents are our friends and that's on a lot of trust issues from past events. My mum always says, *"show me a friend and I'll tell you who you are."* That is such a powerful phrase and she's totally correct, friends either make or break your personality. At the end of day, it's important to know what kind of friends or people you are surrounding yourself with. Perhaps, if they are toxic, then you're going to be toxic too and if they are God-fearing then without a doubt, you're going to follow along.

You can have all the company in the world and still feel disconnected. Still feel numb. Friendship is not an aesthetic. A relationship is not an aesthetic. It actually takes a lot of priority—it requires special attention. And if you give it too much attention, more than God, you already know it, He will take it away. Your relationship with God is also not an aesthetic and definitely not just a routine to follow, that's a very important priority and if you don't have that in the bag then I would recommend you fix that. *God's company is enough.* and you would *realize* that, only when it's fixed.

God will send the right friends or partner into your life who will be able to love you genuinely and love you as God loves the church. In the time being though, continue to focus on your walk with God and rather prepare yourself for those people or that partner God has planned for you. Since God cares for your soul so much, He really wants a positive and respectful influence around you. *Iron sharpens iron* and it's very important to note that the right people will lead you into the right places.

THE MISFORTUNE OF AN UNCLEAN BLEEDING WOMAN (MARK 5:25–34)

Can you imagine bleeding for a period of twelve years? In Mark's gospel, an unidentified woman was unwell and had been suffering for a long time. Her illness has also isolated her from others. She was ritually filthy. She was unable to accompany the other women to the temple. Even at home, she couldn't sit where other people sat, since it would make them unclean. If she walked out in public, others would have known she was filthy, so that didn't bother her. Can you imagine not being able to be touched or even looked at without disgusted glances for a period of twelve years? This woman was yearning to be free of her loneliness. Can you imagine how brave it had to be to quietly touch the hem of Jesus' cloak? Can you imagine how much bravery it needed to respond to Jesus?

> Mark 5:33 Then the woman, knowing what had happened to her, came and fell at his feet and, trembling with fear, told him the whole truth.

When you are accustomed to being secluded for a long time, it is quite difficult to reach out and connect with others, but she was healed when she overcame her fear. Some of us suffer from insecurity, especially while comparing ourselves to other people. An insecurity I suffered from was my nose and my voice. My nose has been one of my biggest insecurities since I knew myself. I was always picked on for it, it was the first thing people saw because it was so . . . well . . . big. It's not the best nose ever honestly, it's not similarly shaped like Gigi Hadid's or the Kardashians but when Jesus came in and made me understand my worth, I *realized* that He created me, the God of the Universe and thinks of me as beautiful and not a single person can take that away from me.

I am also a lead worshiper in my dad's church, so my voice is kind of a big deal. I started when I was about 10. Honestly speaking, I wasn't the best singer. I was pretty badly off at the start. Nonetheless, my worship was honest and very genuine because I really love God and my purest intention was to bless Him. I have always had that love and passion for Him, especially after growing up in a Christ-loving home. I was put down because of my voice and the way I sounded, my voice was said to be too high, childish and annoying. The leader of our ministry wasn't nice to me at all either, I also never mentioned any details or anything to my parents because I thought she was right. As a child, seeing the person in charge like a teacher or someone in authority who is supposed to be a role model to others, you'd start thinking, "What's wrong with me?" She glared and gossiped to everyone about the way I sounded, I would've heard about it too and as expected, it would really hurt me. It happened for a couple years, right up until I was 16, *everything changed,* and I got exceedingly better and well-seasoned, everything basically worked out for good. I'm a soprano as expected and also, the only one on our team. Even if it was hard for me to understand at the beginning why all of this was happening, God's plans worked for the greater good.

It's kind of the same concept for the woman with the issue of blood. She was suffering from insecurity and fear. God met her where she lived, and as a result, she endured a spiritual transformation. But did you notice Jesus' reaction to her? *Jesus said to her, "Daughter, your faith has made you whole."* I could just imagine how gentle and loving He was to her and I could also imagine how intimidating the experience was for her too. Imagine how nobody wanted anything to do with her and your thinking as a normal imperfect human would, "God would never want to touch me." Then He did, without the slightest hesitation. That's the God we serve. A perfect, loving, kind and gentle God, who does not care about your flaws one bit.

You might be driven to believe that the cause of your loneliness is because of your insecurity and what people think of you all the time. Let me advise you, walk with confidence. God knows the plans He has for you and He knows the reason you have that insecurity. You see, I believe that woman bled because God wanted her to be a testimony to many people and amaze people of his goodness. So much so, the woman and the issue of blood was now overlooked and people were more amazed by God's healing. She wasn't made the star of the show, God was. He used her to draw people's attention to Him rather than her insecurity. I can testify today that God has really used me and my voice to draw people to Him—everything worked out for good, just as God planned and has always promised.

DID YOU KNOW JESUS WAS LONELY?

> Matt 27:46 About three in the afternoon Jesus cried out in a loud voice, "Eli, Eli,lema sabachthani?" (Which means "My God, my God, why have you forsaken me?").

These were Christ's final words before dying on the cross. Suffering can be isolating. Dying can be isolating. For Jesus, the Last Supper was a lonely dinner. He was dining with friends He had spent the previous three years pouring into, but he knew that some would deny him and one would intentionally betray him after the meal was finished.

After, he led his friends to a garden to pray. He expressed his heartbreak and requested them to "watch" and pray for him. When they all fell asleep, he had to wake them up three times. Despite the fact that his closest friends surrounded him, Jesus felt alone and abandoned. This group of pals couldn't compensate for the loneliness of the approaching cross. Jesus was abandoned in order to pave the way for us to be restored with God. He gave his life for us.

Imagine, God Himself was lonely. Jesus may have been the loneliest man to ever live on the planet. His father wasn't physically with him. Everyone mocked him, spat on him, rejected him, ignored him, gossiped and spat out mean names to him. Considering who Jesus was, this journey would have started long before his public ministry began. That implies, Jesus can empathize with your loneliness even more than you may have previously imagined.

> Heb 4:15 For we do not have a high priest who is unable to empathize with our weaknesses, but we have One who has been tempted in every way, just as we are—yet He did not sin.

Many of you are suffering from loneliness, maybe because of the loss of someone in your life or someone leaving without saying goodbye, like a parent, a sibling, a boyfriend or maybe a best friend. It gets very lonely when you miss someone and can't do anything about it, in fact it's heartbreaking. It hurts you to live without the person and it hurts you to move on. Many of you are broken by the fact that people just won't stay in your life and just love you, *for you*. Many of you even blame yourself because of this. Jesus is perfect for understanding loneliness. He's been through that and tragically worse than all of us combined. It was like one week everyone was jumping for joy and singing "Hosanna, Hosanna in the highest" and then the next week they just crucified Him which had to have been one of the loneliest moments in history.

Consider how Jesus' childhood had to have been. Do you recall how it felt to want peers? Jesus was totally human, and He too, would have wished for human friendship but missing the sin nature that everyone else possessed and possessing a heavenly nature that no one else possessed, he would have been a very weird individual. That maybe very complicated to understand, so let me elaborate, Jesus wasn't like us who are sinful by nature, allow temptation every now and then and have sinful thoughts. We were born into sin, it is in our nature but Jesus, on the other hand, was without any blemishes and because of this people would have made Him out to be a strange individual. He never fit in, His circle was small, I could simply imagine Him being a teenager and everyone's messing around and doing teenager conundrums and Jesus is just sitting there . . . *unbothered* by the worldly norms. Sin wasn't appealing to Him. It wasn't glamorous to Him; it was wrong and He was well aware of that. So, telling His peers, "Hey bud, that's sin and you shouldn't be dwelling in it." Everyone would probs stare and laugh because they weren't sinless like Jesus was. Their thoughts couldn't match His. He was different. He was perfect. Sinners are tempted to escape when they see holiness. Jesus would have stood out morally like a big flag, never fully comprehended, usually ridiculed or scorned and even by his own family.

The point I'm trying to draw is, out of everyone to ever exist, Jesus definitely understands. Stop shunning Him away too and start talking to Him. He loves you more than anyone ever will in a lifetime combined. Keep the Savior close to you—that way you'll never have to feel alone again.

CHAPTER 3

Wounds of Loneliness

A mental approach

﹡

How could a person even encounter wounds and bruises during a lonely battle? It's merely impossible to have physical wounds during a mental battle, right? Loneliness brings in two things: healing or more brokenness. Healing means to fully get over, forgive and move on to greater things. A lot of the times healing does not just mean physical but also mentally and emotionally. Whether it means a heart break from a relationship or a parent stepping out and never coming back or even a friendship.

I have been through so many friendships that has messed me up completely . . . especially my last one. I went to school with this girl and she was the sweetest most understanding person I had ever met. She was broken but I loved her, she was my best friend and I thought we would have always been friends but frankly, God had other plans in mind. I want you guys to understand that when someone walks out of your life and nobody supports you, time doesn't help or even slightly tries to heal you, trust me, it might feel like that but the trauma from that will never go away. God heals all wounds, no matter how deep, every shape and every size.

You need to begin accepting *responsibility* for yourself. You now have a responsibility to yourself and you have God to complete you. Every day, work to make yourself whole, you won't regret investing in yourself. There's a difference between self-love and vanity in this world. Self-love is worship. Vanity is sin. Look at it this way, you love God and He created you, learn to love and take good care of what He created you to be and whatever purpose He has for you, realize it and fulfill it.

Healing was vital to Jesus' ministry because He saw it as a tangible sign of forgiveness and redemption. Through His personal resurrection, He promised the ultimate glory of the human body, but He predicted that redemption by curing deformed, withered, and crippled limbs and organs. Your healing matters so much to God that Jesus endured near-death suffering all for our healing. Your healing has been compensated for, with Jesus' blood. Never let the devil try to convince you contrary of that.

Sometimes, God puts you through loneliness, for healing. Healing always starts with the decision to follow Jesus and the final decision to walk with Him. In order for us to acquire true wholeness, we must commit completely, just as our Lord did when he stated the greatest commission of God. There must be something you've experienced and it traumatized you— *"hmm, it popped in your head, didn't it?"* I sure pray it did because realizing what broke you is the second step of healing. And finally, it's giving it all to God and allowing him to heal your brokenness. Again, there's nothing that could compare to God and there's nothing He can't do. He's perfect for your healing.

Loneliness, most of the time, actually contributes to a lot of damage, you are very vulnerable by yourself. In my culture, we don't leave our parents for college. The island is small, consisting of our own Universities, so we get to live with our parents. Some kids are brave enough to leave and move away but most people usually make their lives here— I mean, who wants to not-live on an island right? My point is, it's only after we get married, we move on from our parents' house. I honestly think it's safest especially for a girl-child because her father is her covering and protection. Sons, also need protection and responsibility learned from their father in order to take in a bride and protect her as her father would have.

What I mean by loneliness causing damage is that—there's room for sin and room for vulnerability. Without a parent, kids get carried away. It doesn't matter if "you're 18 and mature" When sin grips you, trust me it grips you hard. It may not apply to everyone but the devil really has you there sometimes, not to worry though because when Jesus steps in there is no room for sin and vulnerability only love and direction.

In this chapter, I want to share with you five different things that take place during your loneliness to look out for. But before I do, I would like to point out that everyone experiences 'the lonely' differently and some things may not apply to you but the information can be noted and feel free to pray against these things before it actually happens to you. Remember, that you are never alone if you do experience these scenarios and God hears you and is willing to heal you in this.

THE GREAT DEPRESSION

For the past two years, I have been taking psychology courses and let me tell you I have had a better understanding about the way I feel sometimes and the way people who experience mood and depressive disorders actually feel. I understand way too well what it's like dwelling in sorrow. I don't have depression, but I do feel sad and I will have you know it is my most hated emotion, right in front of anger. Sorrow happens sometimes, while depression is very much long term. When I feel sad it's mostly for reasons like school, heartbreak from previous friendships, arguments with my parents, when I'm sick and or maybe when I do something embarrassing (which I do quite often). I can happily say that praying and intimately spending time with God has really been the reason why I haven't fallen prey to this disease.

Depression is a condition characterized by a poor mood and reluctance to activities. Depression is a mental and cognitive condition that affects a person's thoughts and emotions, conduct, ambition, sentiments, and well-being. Loneliness can be very demotivating and painful. It brings about a different person, it's not the same child your parents raised and the sad part is it's very hidden. Whenever the storms of depression hit, it can feel helpless and gloomy. Sometimes storms feel larger than others, yet they don't ever seem to stop.

> Proverbs 12:25 Anxiety weighs down the heart, but a kind word cheers it up.

The Bible didn't necessarily say the word "depression"; the disorder only came to the light by doctors in the 20th century. Sad, right? From the beginning of the Bible down to even King David, a number of figures in the Bible appear to have suffered from depression.

Storytime

I actually remember a guy who had a bit of depression himself, Moses. He actually went through this "gloomy wilderness" period multiple times over his lengthy life. Moses had been entrusted by God with carrying Israel out of Egypt from slavery and to the Promised Land, a duty he didn't even want, but God urged on it. We all know what it feels like to wash the dishes when we don't want to, and this task was treacherous in itself. He'd do whatever God told him time and time again, as he should, only to meet criticism, protest, and disapproval from his folks, who were displeased and intimidated for the slightest problem. I mean the poor guy was leading you out of a kind of great depression, like, why complain? Then after, the Israelites yelled at him in the wilderness, Moses got fed up of their whines and pleaded out to the Lord. I can honestly say, good for him because I'd be pretty pressed as well.

> Num 11:14–15 I cannot carry all these people by my-self; the burden is too heavy for me. 15 If this is how you are going to treat me, please go ahead and kill me—if I have found favor in your eyes—and do not let me face my own ruin."

Secondly, we have the famous Jeremiah who had been through depression and as explained before, loneliness can cause depression. He too was also rejected, scorned by his people, impoverished, and lonely, fought with depression throughout his life. At one of his lowest points, he cursed the day he was born (Jeremiah 20:14) and cried out, "Why did I ever come out of the womb to see difficulty and sorrow and to end my days in shame?" not to mention that he was destined to be lonely.

And lastly, Judas Iscariot, I mean, we can clearly see why he was depressed . . . he died of guilt and so he hung himself. Imagine betraying Jesus and I'm only saying that because we do that every day. We hurt God sometimes and it hurts God to see us dwelling in so much sin and then reaping sadness or long-term guilt from it. Especially when he promised joy. The devil wants you to commit that sinful act of dwelling in habitual sin, so when it's done, he is free to crawl into your mind and mess with your security in God. He might fill your mind with thoughts like: "Look at how disgusting you are, you sinful pig! God will never forgive you or love you after this." He might even drive you to believe you're the only one stuck in this sin and you're going to rot in Hell forever. I can safely say that God does not want that, He wants you in Heaven with Him and He wants you to know He overcame sin a long time ago and saved us from "the Great depression"

From these stories we can grasp that these men were significantly some of the loneliest men in the Bible, Moses and God, it was just Jeremiah and his 'lonely' calling and then there's Judas, who betrayed God, made a deal with the devil and has committed suicide. As we may very well know depression is the root of suicide, hence the reason, he gave up and decided to hang himself. It is not labeled as a sin, but rather as a worldly adversity, similar to oppression or even deprivation and poverty, which Jesus himself said would always be with us.

Matt 26:11 The poor you will always have with you, but you will not always have me.

ANTIDOTE -

Remember when Moses said, "I cannot carry all these people by myself; the burden is too heavy for me." God never wanted him or you to carry around any burdens. He specifically said to trust Him and He will do the rest, yet still we believe we have to do everything ourselves when we have a God to help us along the way. Never fight this battle with your own strength. Let God do it. You do not have to walk on eggshells with God, He got this and He never disappoints. It has absolutely no hold on you and it has no space in your life. The demon behind this disease is surely lying to you and feeding you ungodly thoughts. Bring your sorrows to God and make your petitions large you are speaking to the King of all Kings and Lord of Lords.

A prayer I wrote for you faithful individuals suffering with this chronic disease:

Dear God,
I just want to thank you for the individual that is reading this book and is fighting this hidden disease called depression. God, I pray for resilience in this time and strength to move forward. Jesus, even as they go to sleep at night, I pray for proper rest Lord. I pray for motivation to even go to school and focus on their classes, Lord, you never made us fail. You created us to prosper, elevate and succeed. Lord your promises still stand to this day and I thank you for that. I pray your holy spirit will continue to direct them to your Kingdom Purpose. Lord, you said that there may be sorrow and pain at night but joy comes in the morning. I pray against the spirit of suicide and every person that is struggling with it, that spirit has no hold on their life and I break that curse in the name of Jesus. Dad, I thank you again for who you are and what you're about to do. In Jesus' mighty and precious name, I pray, Amen.

AN ANXIOUS HEART

Many of us have experienced anxiety. Anxiety is the physiological reaction of the body to perceived threat or danger. It generates a racing heart, accelerated breathing, butterflies in the stomach, and a surge of energy, as well as emotional responses such as increased anxieties, concerns, or compulsive and obsessive worrying. We experience anxiety for many reasons such as getting scared when God asks us to do something, stage fright, around large groups of people and even to write exams. I have experienced this way too often in my life, so much that I had literally become numb to it. Usually, I would just cry but now I just sit and stare at my walls

Recently, my dad asked me to fill in and help preach for him on Sundays because he had a business trip. The first Sunday I was pretty fine and I guess it was because I was just super excited. Then the second Sunday—let's just say the devil did not like it when I preached God's word. A variety of things were happening to me from terrible dreams of demons in my room—while they were sticking their long disgusting nails into my throat and body, to constant hypotension and a very bad cold and a fever. Which were all signs of anxiety. Demons naturally feed on fear. Demons even get jealous as well, so they reside in your home and life, relationships too as if it's their own but I'll speak more on them later.

Storytime

I'm here to tell you guys that anxiety is a huge lie and it should not have any hold in your life. When Elijah was scolded while expecting to prevail, he became apprehensive. His high dreams were dashed, and he got ill at heart. Elijah had been the embodiment of spiritual bravery up until this time. He now collapses, flees when Jezebel threatened his existence and when Israel most needs his leadership, maybe missing the opportunity for national atonement, and turns suicidal. He was plagued by spiritual anxiety, a type of worry that is associated with devotion to God. Elijah's worry, like that of many other biblical heroes, serves as a reminder that being committed to God does not guarantee to insulate us from uneasiness.

The Bible never indicated that us Christians will always be happy. God never said it would have been easy, He just said that *it'll all be worth it in the end.* You will be persecuted and tormented in different ways because of His righteousness' sake. Fear will come. That's okay though, because God's got you guys right at the palm of his hands.

ANTIDOTE

Don't let fear grip you. Whenever I'm appointed to preach or worship at my church and I begin to feel that surge of anxiety packing in like a tsunami, I pray. I pray as if I've never prayed before. I use anxiety as an *alert* from God, to pray and rest in God's presence. I would go to the other side of the building and start crying my eyes out to God, I tell him what it is that I feel and to make it go away for as long as I can. For the boys especially, reading this, it is perfectly okay to cry out to your Father. It's not a sign of weakness that people make it out to be. Trust me He's waiting for you to tell Him about your fears and worry.

Us Christians, also need to come to the realization that you are in constant battle with the devil. Keep praying and keep covering yourself with the blood. The devil has no victory when God's in the picture, he is bound for loss. I cannot begin to fathom how much God really cares about His kids. I really can't. I honestly just know from scripture, just like how he wept for Lazarus knowing he would come back alive, He still cried. Now that's love. God wants to heal you from this fear. He wants you to stop living in so much fear. My main advice is to keep on praying.

If you also know a brother or sister that is struggling with anxiety, remember God's word, a cheerful word cheers up the heart. Learn to encourage your brothers and sisters in unity. Don't watch them drown or don't say you're busy and have problems too. Jesus never said that and He too struggled with loneliness and fear of dying on the cross, He was human too. Ask yourself what would Jesus do? Jesus would've loved, encouraged, nurtured and supported.

A prayer I wrote for you faithful individuals struggling with fear and anxiety:

> Dear Dad,
>
> I come before you today in perfect adoration for everything you have done for us. I thank you Lord for waking us up and still promising us a future during this painful season. I lift up your sons and daughters of Christ and I pray, God, that you continue to nurture them, encourage them and love them. Lord, give them the strength to get up and pray and the desire to seek you more and more every day. I pray against this demon that is tormenting their lives and minds with fear and pain. I rebuke every assignment of the enemy over their lives and I pray for comfort and a cheerful spirit. In Jesus' mighty name, Amen.

MENTAL INSANITY AND SUICIDAL TENDENCIES

We have all thought about it, "Maybe if I just die, my problems will go away." I have never tried anything but I have thought of it. Let's not kid ourselves, life is hard, it's demotivating, tiring and all we really want to do is be with Jesus at the end of the day. That's okay. It's pretty normal to grieve being with Jesus and living in Heaven. But loneliness makes a person overthink the situation so much that they end up with the suicidal tendencies and it drives them to insanity since we know God wouldn't appreciate us doing that to ourselves.

Imagine you doing this terrible act to yourself, you end up in God's throne room and Jesus turns to you in complete shock and says, "What are you doing here, Rebecca? You weren't supposed to be here until the next 57 years." You then, have no answer which is quite embarrassing. He continues, "I wasn't done with you darling, why did you do that? what am I to do with you for the next 57 years?" let's finalize that that's *totally embarrassing*.

It is quite clear that suicide stems from depression, obviously. People who are depressed cannot think clearly compared to a stable individual. When I feel sad, I never make critical or life-changing decisions, according to my philosophy. When one is melancholy, life constantly appears to be bleak. The majority of the folks I know who have committed suicide are despondent. In fact, I believe that, with a few instances, no one attempts suicide unless they are unhappy.

Suicide is a very controversial topic. I don't like giving my opinions without proper evidence so what I am about to say is more objective than rather being subjective, this is as easy as I can explain it:

In your defense, we love Jesus and we believe and accept Him as our Lord and savior. Why would He send me to Hell? And this may be right, it makes sense but God doesn't actually send people to Hell. We chose hell as a part of our free will. Yes, He is also our only judge and yes, He gets to make that decision but He wishes that none should ever perish but that all persons come to repentance and have everlasting life.

> 2 Pet 3:9 The Lord is not slow in keeping his promise, as some understand slowness. Instead, he is patient with you, not wanting anyone to perish, but everyone to come to repentance.

Secondly, when you commit suicide, that's basically killing or murdering yourself. Murder is a sin. The wages of sin is death and the ten commandments stated that "Thou shall not kill." The penalty for sin like murder is Hell. Committing a sin is a *choice*. Committing suicide is also a choice. Not forgetting, that when a person commits suicide, that spirit of suicide remains in the generation and by extension the generations to come.

If you have doubt based on going to hell after suicide, I recommend you listen to the Holy Spirit and make sure it's Him, none of us wants Hell for eternity, that's even worse than life on earth. God doesn't want you to perish.

Storytime

The Roman government deported John on the lonely island of Patmos because of his proclamation of the gospel. On the island of Patmos, John heard communications from Jesus to the churches as well as visions of the end times. It was there, John began to write the book of Revelation.

Patmos served as a haven for criminals and political prisoners. Inmates were allowed to wander the small island with relative freedom, although most had to provide their own basic necessities and were guarded against fleeing by Roman soldiers. Many died as a result of dampness, deadly attacks by other prisoners, or malnutrition. According to legend, John's friends and supporters in Ephesus sent basic necessities to him on the isle, which is how he endured.

The isle of Patmos is quite unnecessary and unimportant. God chooses the most insignificant things in this world to prove even the wisest and strongest people wrong. So that when people come before him, they go to His throne room humbly.

> 1 Cor 1:27–29 But God chose the foolish things of the world to shame the wise; God chose the weak things of the world to shame the strong. 28 God chose the lowly things of this world and the despised things— and the things that are not—to nullify the things that are, 29 so that no one may boast before him.

The island did not draw any attention to God, it had nothing to do with Him. What was important to God is that John was there and He entrusted him with His greatest prophecies. That's what mattered to God. God does not care about what you are surrounded by. He doesn't care about your messy room and chairs full of dirty clothes because it does not define you. He cares about you. He is saying that regardless of the loneliness in your room and the suicidal tendencies that you encounter within it, He wants you to know that He sees *you* not your sin. He hates the sin, *not* the sinner. He despises the problems in your life, not *you*.

ANTIDOTE

John found Himself on Patmos because He loved Jesus and was trying to spread the gospel. You too, may be in the same situation and may feel as if you're banished with your mental health problems by yourself with no one to understand. God never promised it'll be easy but He did promise it'll be worth it when you wait and trust Him.

My advice as a sister in Christ, keep on praying. Remember that you're not alone and God has presented a support system. If you know that you are struggling with suicide and you're having serious tendencies, please speak to your pastor or a counselor to help you. Help is available for you, don't feel the need to try to hide your pain, or struggle through, on your own. And remember through everything Jesus understands and He is good and His mercies endures forever. Allow God to shower you with joy and don't push Him away. Don't turn your back. He wants you and He wants you to be with Him one day in Heaven.

A prayer I wrote for you faithful individuals struggling with suicidal tendencies and are going insane over it:

Dear Dad,

I thank you again for these wonderful youths today. I thank you for helping them reach thus far in this book. I pray to God that you will continue to watch over them. God, you said that the weapon may be formed against them but it will not prosper. I pray against the spirit of suicide. God this demon took over this entire generation. Youths are dying every day, falling prey to this. Father, I pray for your protection over them and for your holy spirit to speak too and through them. I give you all of the praise, the honor and glory in Jesus' name, Amen.

DYSMORPHIA

Body dysmorphic disorder is a psychological issue in which you can't stop obsessing about one or more perceived imperfections in your image. It is an imperfection that seems trivial or is invisible to everybody else, but you. However, you may dodge numerous social interactions because you are uncomfortable, embarrassed, or nervous.

If you have body dysmorphic disorder, you obsess over your appearance and physical image, examining the mirror, cleaning, or seeking validation periodically throughout the day often for many hours. Your recognized imperfection and repeating actions give you severe distress and have an influence on your capacity to perform activities of daily living. Boy or girl, if you suffer with this, this verse is yours...

> 1 Pet 3:3–4 Your beauty should not come from outward adornment, such as elaborate hairstyles and the wearing of gold jewelry or fine clothes. 4 Rather, it should be that of your inner self, the unfading beauty of a gentle and quiet spirit, which is of great worth in God's sight.

Outward appearance is something society craves, especially out of influencers. You guys realize that these influencers get either surgery done or use filters and apps to shape their face and body most of the time, right? Especially, to enhance their outward appearance and or cover it with even more makeup. Aside from that, some were even interviewed and spoke about their unhealthy and restrictive relationship with food and would usually work out more after that to achieve their body goals and keep their surgery efforts in shape. I'm here to tell you what God says about it. God hates that we treat ourselves and our bodies this way. In fact, eating disorders are incompatible with God's design for us. Binging, purging, and starvation are not God's methods of treating the body.

I was a huge fan of one of those celebrities, I was a fan since I was 9 actually. She was always very beautiful and I honestly thought that's how she looked as a normal human being. I thought that God favouritized, which definitely isn't true. The way her body was shaped, her eyes were big with long eyelashes, full lips, a straight nose and gorgeous blonde hair, it had made me so insecure. Not realizing—it was just makeup, she had botox, a nose job, eyelash extensions and a full-on eating disorder.

> 1 Cor 10:31 So whether you eat or drink or whatever you do, do it all for the glory of God.

With every inch of concern in my heart, please, do not go destroying your diet, metabolism and mental health for the appreciation of society. It's not worth it. In everything you do make sure it glorifies God. You think eating 500 calories a day, pleases God? It doesn't. Please, understand that God made you perfect. God sees no flaw in you. He ignores your sin, your past, He is more than able to bypass the insecurity of your little muffin top or nose. To top that off, He created you just the way He wanted you and made no mistakes in doing so. He's God, *God doesn't make mistakes.*

> 1 Cor 6:19–20 Do you not know that your bodies are temples of the Holy Spirit, who is in you, whom you have received from God? You are not your own; 20 you were bought at a price. Therefore, honor God with your bodies.

I know that it is very challenging. Especially in your loneliness, there's little to no validation or motivation, it's just you. During this time, your little insecurities get the best of you. Repetitively counting your macros or calories or obsessing over workouts to burn off those calories. One of the worst things for a youth, is that you have time. Time can be painful and long. It causes a lot of disadvantages, leaves a lot of room for demons to mess with you and frustrate you. Kind of like, during the pandemic, we have time, there's just online school, work, always home in this little room. It creates more havoc than you think. We may be safe from covid but not from our minds but Jesus came to set the captives free, we can have life and life more abundantly. The Bible says that…

> 1 Tim 4:8 For physical training is of some value, but godliness has value for all things, holding promise for both the present life and the life to come

It's okay to be healthy, don't obsess over it though but this scripture indicates that godliness is more important. Godliness is when a person is not secular. The person is Godly when they pray, read their Bible and stay away from sin. It doesn't matter your outside appearance; *God looks at your heart* according to your deeds.

ANTIDOTE

The Bible talks about something called Unity. I try my best to be an example to my youth ministry when it comes to this. Unity is important to God. For us Christians, it shouldn't matter race, gender, size or religion even. It doesn't matter who they are, Jesus still loves them and you should too. Jesus sat with the sinners and conversated. People may not refer to me as a friend but if I know you, automatically I will call you friend. That's just my personality, I love to show off God's love and I like making people feel as though they belong—I know what it feels like to feel neglected, I won't blame you if you do either because as Christians we are supposed to stand out and not fit in. I guess what I am trying to say is to just be kind because you never know what someone may be going through. They may be starving, depressed and isolated, pain is an understatement.

Don't undervalue another person's problems. Insecurity is common. Dysphoria is prominent and rampaging in youths. Eating disorders are flying through the roof. Be kind. Be one. Thrive in unity with one another. Don't put them down for their body. Don't say mean things. Calling someone "fat", "ugly", "dumb" or other mean things promotes body disorders. Just be kind and teach your kids kindness too. It goes a long way.

Secondly, talk to someone older. Unite with other youths. You never know, they may be suffering with the same things or worse. The Bible says that iron sharpens iron, you can be a huge inspiration to amaze people about Jesus' healing.

A prayer I wrote for those suffering with dysphoria.

Dear dad,

I thank you, for each person reading this. I thank you for the wonderful people they are and are prospering to be. I pray for healing over each person's mind. I pray that this active spirit of dysphoria will be dismissed and sent back to where it came from. I pray for strength to recover. I pray for your hand to be over them and for your word to be prominent in their lives so they don't forget you love them. In Jesus' name, Amen.

SEXUAL IMMORALITY

I know that most of you all are in your youth, let's face it every single teenager faces loneliness, even if they have all of the friends in the world or are in a relationship. It still gets lonely. In these lonely times, where we have time and freedom, sin finds its way into our lives, especially youths. I'd know, I have a youth ministry and very in particular they face a lot of temptation when it comes to sexual sin. In this part of your life, your hormones are acting up and you start "feeling." You start having crushes, little boyfriends and girlfriends, you may want to touch them or even hold their hands and share kisses. Whether or not you are single . . . sexual sin happens. There are ways teenagers find to exert the excitement, either through sexual conversations on Snapchat or through partying and hooking up.

Before I proceed to the meat on this topic, I have a strong reminder that God wants you to have sex more than you want to have sex. For biblical purposes of course, multiplying on earth and creating beautiful and Christ-like generations.

With regards to sexual immorality, there are different forms of it: masturbation, pornography, smut reading and sexual intercourse. Masturbation is basically done by one person, yourself, it's when you touch yourself to feed your fleshly desire. Pornography is when you look at other people committing sexual acts through some kind of device or website, which on the other hand spoils and rips God's normalcy for the gift of sex. Smut reading, now very popular, is when you read graphic scenes in books which gives people the idea that BDSM, for example, is okay outside of marriage. Which also spoils the reputation of sex, especially for males, sex is worship and its sacred. It's not a game or a one-night stand. It's specially designed by God for married couples to create convenance between them, it creates oneness and it's also almost like imprinting on someone forever.

Sexual intercourse is the act between two individuals that are in love, more specifically should be done by married couples *only*. The devil has twisted and tampered with sex so much that individuals get carried away with it. He uses sexual impurities as a way to distract young people from the things of God. These sexual acts activate the hormone called dopamine. Eventually, any sexual act you become addicted too becomes a routine or a habit in your life, causing you to become addicted to sexual activities. It causes your bodies to want more and more dopamine until the satisfaction coming from the acts isn't enough. Then finally, as you grow older and get married it becomes hard for your wife or husband to satisfy you. It brings in catastrophe in marriages. It creates a lot of insecurity and loneliness between partners.

For the single folks, meaning the ones who aren't in a relationship—it is vital for you to stay pure because your body is a temple for the holy spirit to reside in. It wasn't clearly written in the Bible but sexual immorality is a sin. It doesn't only destroy marriages, simple friendships and relationships between people, but also, *yourself*. In fact, it's the only sin that is committed against your own body. So, if Satan can't destroy you on his own and with his own power, he'll try to convince you into destroying your own self. Same goes for every other sin too, he uses some of them to get to you in order to destroy yourself. Masturbation and pornography are the two most prominent sins in sexual immorality for the singles. In your alone time, temptations lurk in and out of nowhere causing you to feel things and have certain desires. That's where alone time *with* God becomes important. If you can't be trusted to stay in a room by yourself without thinking about masturbating or watching pornography, that's a red flag.

> 1 Cor 6:18–20 Flee from sexual immorality. All other sins a person commits are outside the body, but whoever sins sexually, sins against their own body. 19 Do you not know that your bodies are temples of the Holy Spirit, who is in you, whom you have received from God? You are not your own; 20 you were bought at a price. Therefore, honor God with your bodies.

For my people in relationships, meaning boyfriends and girlfriends of any age. Although, I believe being in a relationship too young isn't the best choice because it becomes a real distraction in your lives. Nonetheless, life happens for the best of us, so if you are in a relationship at a younger age, no judgment here, stuff happens and that's okay. Moving along, when you're in a relationship with someone, boundaries are important, you get to create those boundaries from where you are comfortable, to where you are not or where you feel as if the Holy Spirit is convicting you against certain things that you do in your relationships. Not forgetting, that we have to *ask* God for the Holy Spirit to come into our lives and then you will be able to clearly feel conviction or be aware of when the Holy Spirit tries to warn you about a certain act. The Hebrew word *yakah* expresses the idea of conviction. It means "to argue with," "to prove," "to correct." God likes to be invited into your life, He's a king, He has respect, well . . . He pretty much created respect. Bottomline, is He wants to be welcomed into your life and from here, you will be able to pinpoint what you think is right and wrong according to the Holy Spirit.

Why are boundaries so important? It's because men and women are wired very differently. Men get more feelings than women do, just by the slight touch or watch, temptations come marching in. Men are attracted by what they see, with that being said, respect your boyfriend and dress modestly. Women, on the other hand, once they're in love, love bombed and are sweet-talked daily will certainly feel something. Women cave by what they hear. Sweet words and acts of service or gestures, for instance. This is where sin lies, when we follow our "feeling" or "emotions" and not God. Relationships can be difficult especially if you're Christian. You will crave each other and eventually cave if you're not *careful*. You can set boundaries like: hand holding, kissing (*which is debatable)*, some people wait until the right moment or on their wedding day, sharing or receiving long hugs, but only for a certain amount of time or for some relationships *'don't touch at all.'* I know that's tough, but if you guys really can't control yourselves, it's for the best. The way I see it—you don't want to go ruining your wedding night, do you?

> 1 Thess 4:3–5 It is God's will that you should be sanctified: that you should avoid sexual immorality; 4 that each of you should learn to control your own body in a way that is holy and honorable, 5 not in passionate lust like the pagans, who do not know God;
>
> 1 Thess 4:7 For God did not call us to be impure, but to live a holy life.

God gives man and woman the delight and pleasure of sexual interactions within the confines of marriage, and the Bible is unequivocal about the need of keeping sexual purity within the confines of that union between man and wife (Ephesians 5:31). Humans are fully aware of the gratifying impact of this God-given gift, but they have extended it well beyond marriage and into almost every setting. The secular world's concept of "if it feels good, do it" has permeated civilizations, particularly in the Western areas, to the point that sexual purity is regarded as outdated and unneeded.

The way I see it, it's an entire cycle just waiting to happen:

You feel lonely → temptations lurk → you commit the act → you feel good for a couple of seconds → then you feel terrible for disobeying God's design for sex → depression comes driving in and anxiety for your salvation and life.

Storytime-

I want you to know that when you commit these acts, you open doorways for demons and you lose blessings. I don't know if you're familiar with the Nephilim, before in the early days when Lucifer fell from Heaven and came to Earth with a third of the angels they use to have sexual intercourse with humans which they birthed and were called Nephilim. Nephilim basically means half human half demon. When you masturbate or commit any other sexual act, you open doorways for demons to come into your life and you will start experiencing dreams. Better known as, "wet dreams" these dreams are basically demons molesting you in your sleep. This means that a demon is now attached to you and if you are in a relationship, I am so sorry, but that demon is more than likely jealous of you and your relationship. Your relationship will never see its way because of it. Obviously, *only* Jesus can fix that, don't rely on your own strengths to heal your relationship or yourself.

Believers know that God's laws and discipline are a reflection of His love for us. Following His instructions can only benefit us throughout our stay on Earth. By being sexually pure prior to marriage, we minimize hormonal entanglements that may have a detrimental impact on future relationships and marriages. Furthermore, by maintaining the marriage bed pure, we can feel unconditional love for our partners, which is only topped by God's immense love for us.

ANTIDOTE

Firstly, in order to combat the sin—tell someone you trust, confession is good for the soul. If you have a trusted friend or you can even talk to a Christian guardian or mentor, your youth leader or pastor even, talk to them and I'm sure that they'll give you their best advice. Call them when you are tempted or if you mess up, allow the person to keep you accountable. At this point the enemy just wants you in the depths of loneliness and isolation.

> Prov 11:14 For lack of guidance a nation falls, but victory is won through many advisers.

Secondly, do not entertain it, use it as an alarm to talk to God. Start praying. Start interceding. Start meditating in God's word. Instead of focusing on the sin, focus on Him. Find a distraction (anything but your phones) listen to music from your boombox, find an artistic hobby or do 50 pushups and worship at the same time. Trust me it works. Go into prayer and fasting, make those petitions large unto God, *He hears you.* Strengthen the relationship you have with God. There's nothing to be ashamed about with God defending you.

Thirdly, it is vital to replace your habitual sin with Christ. Make sure that everything you do is Christly and put on the full armour of God to fight this. Remember, if your heart and mind isn't completely in this you won't do your best work. The verse below discusses that when you empty yourself and demons leave, they come back eventually, and they return worse than before. This is why you must continue to fill yourself with God and His words of wisdom, it will strengthen you and help build resilience when the temptation becomes heavy. You cannot rely on your own strength, it'll run out. Rely on God and His strength, He is enough.

> Matt 12:43–45 "When an impure spirit comes out of a person, it goes through arid places seeking rest and does not find it. 44 Then it says, 'I will return to the house I left.' When it arrives, it finds the house unoccupied, swept clean and put in order. 45 Then it goes and takes with it seven other spirits more wicked

than itself, and they go in and live there. And the final
condition of that person is worse than the first. That
is how it will be with this wicked generation."

Fourthly, get rid of the bad company. You read that correct,
I mean the friends that encourage you to do wrong and invade
themselves in sexual acts. They aren't helping you; they will make
it worse. Do yourself a favour and keep some distance. Your salvation is more important than a group of friends that aren't Christ-
like and Godly.

Lastly, you dare not give up on yourself. Nobody is perfect.
You may have sinned today; you may have sinned before or maybe
you're reading this and you're tempted right now. Don't give up
or give into sin. I promise those few seconds of pleasures are not
worth it, especially by the fact that God has so much prepared for
you, so many other greater bigger things that don't include this. He
wants you to be free in Him and if you do make a mistake, He is
more than able to restore every piece of brokenness inside of you.
He doesn't hate you and He doesn't think differently about you.
There are solutions. Him dying on that cross created some hope
and solution for our sin. He paid our debt already all you have to
do is make the right decision.

*I wrote a prayer for those of you who's struggle involved sexual
immorality*

Dear God,

I lift every single person who is fighting this secretive
and destructive spirit and even generational curse in
their lives that prominently involves this sexual sin.
And I ask Jesus that you heal every person that is
fighting this storm. I pray you strengthen them like
you did to David in order to fight and succeed this gi-
ant in their life. I thank you God for every amazing
person reading this book and I pray you continue to
teach them through the knowledge you presented
them with, in Jesus' mighty and precious name,
Amen.

WITCHCRAFT AND MANIFESTATIONS

Hear me out, this is actually getting out of hand by a lot of young adults. They are normalizing the laws of attraction and much much worse. Have you guys ever come across this on Tik Tok or YouTube where it's promoting, like: manifesting blue eyes or an hourglass body shape or even manifesting my crush to like me and your seeing kids writing persons names on paper, putting their lipstick and spraying it with perfume then burning it? That is called black magic and the law of attraction, better known as witchcraft.

Here's a personal example of how easy it is to get yourself in trouble. A few years ago, I wanted to go vegan and at first my dad was just observing the way I was eating and when it got too far and I wasn't eating properly, he finally stopped me and said, "Rebecca, whatever it is you think you're doing by 'saving the animals' is completely ridiculous and it is a *cult*." Don't just read the rest of this chapter in shock the whole time, Google it, watch podcasts on it and do your own research.

Veganism is the adoration of animals based on the mistaken belief that when animals are appropriately utilized for food, they are tortured. Vegans believe they are smarter and more virtuous than the overall population, and they severely criticize the writers and followers of the Scriptures, who provide humankind with healthful and verified recommendations from God about the usage of animals for nourishment. Veganism is a particularly dangerous ideology and cult because it goes straight-up, opposing God and His perfect reasoning with a self-righteous zeal that would kill everyone and everything – even their precious animals – if they gained power. Veganism is insane and contradictory in this way.

This is not to imply that everyone should be compelled to consume meat or that they ought not to be able to select what they dine. Not everyone will be required to marry, so the same holds true for someone's nutrition. Veganism, on the other hand, is a forceful doctrine that denies people' personal freedom, subtly preying on people's sense of right and wrong by characterizing them as butchers if they consume meat. Admittedly, it was the land of milk and honey, not tofu, cashew cheese and soy, that God granted the people of Israel as their tremendous inherited benefit.

I was totally into veganism in the long run also, which is scary. The devil literally almost snatched me right there just by not knowing what I was doing. Eating meat is God's design for our diet. We need it for protein. Look up the benefits of protein from real meat. Yes, you can get protein from legumes or even some other foods and staples but it isn't the same.

Law of attraction has people thinking that they are better than God or perhaps they are God. This philosophy is clear blasphemy of any kind. Please do not blindly follow this, there is one true God. Many teenagers are doing this to pass exams and make themselves look and feel good, this isn't the way God intended you to do it. Please, be aware that Satan is a shark waiting to consume you at any moment.

Another example I can say was pretty freakish as well was this one time I put on this movie on Netflix, "Don't kill me." My niece whom I was babysitting, took one glimpse of the TV and sprung out of her seat and rushed to me crying. It dawned on me for a second—"wait . . . is this movie demonic?" indeed it was a horror movie. It wasn't until I prayed with her, she calmed down. For those of you who are lost, horror movies drag in demons and are demonic portholes for demons to come into your house and life. The thing is I was unaware at the moment that it was a horror movie, until I googled it. Be careful of what you watch and invite into your homes. It's easy for demons to crawl in at any moment without realization. We are at that point where demons are flooding the earth more than anything and is monitoring your house, your family and your soul, waiting to sneak in and grab you.

How does this apply to loneliness? To your surprise, when teenagers are alone, they get themselves into a lot of crazy stuff and secrecy to occupy themselves. Young Christians are unaware because the adults aren't teaching them that these things exist. Manifestations and witchcraft are everywhere, social media and in front of their eyes and yours. Evil eyes, yoga and dream-catchers are all a part of this. You don't need an evil-eye God will protect you. You don't need yoga to be healthy or have a great digestion because cardio and aerobic exercises exist. There's much more options than yoga for exercise. If you research yoga, research will tell you the background of it and that it summons demons. And finally, you most definitely don't need a dream-catcher, God is able to heal your sleeping problems and protect you all you really have to do is ask Him.

People will literally try everything else but Jesus, give Him a chance. Witchcraft wasn't his creation. Manifestation was not his plan either. Educate yourself in the things of God and even the things that are not of God.

ANTIDOTE

Research any and everything, and study your Bible and obey God's will. Curiosity is okay, ask your questions and don't be scared of the answers. This one is simple although tough to do, listen the devil is sneaky. Don't give him room. Another key thing is to listen to the Holy Spirit who will convict you, He'll say, "Hey, you should take that movie off or maybe doing this isn't a good idea." It's important to adapt with discernment because it will help guide you and show you what's off God and what isn't. To get the Spirit of Discernment, you simply ask God to give it to you. It is a special gift and it is very useful but bear in mind your gift isn't yours, it is given to you and then you use it to help other people. I like to call it an "Investigator in the Spirit Realm." Also, always cover yourself with the blood of Jesus, every time you come and go. And lastly, talking to your elders as well, who are aware and experienced with and knows of the spirit realm and what it contains is helpful. You never know what you might learn from them.

My prayer to you:

Dear Lord,

Some of your kids are unaware of their actions sometimes and are quite blind to your will and the things of you. I pray that God will make a way for them to see. Open up their eyes and ears to know who you are and you are all powerful. God, for those who are lost in this dimension, I pray that you open up their eyes to see the evil and ungodliness in these things. Father, you have your divine way, in Jesus' name. Amen.

CHAPTER 4

The Attack of Loneliness

When does the devil attack during loneliness?

✳

id you know loneliness can cause heart problems? Like when a couple gets older and are in their last days, let's say the wife dies. Months later, you might notice that the husband fell sick somehow and eventually died. The reason is because he misses his wife so dearly that he fell sick from the depression that came from loneliness and died, grieving her. Loneliness can kill a person. If it doesn't literally kill you. It will kill your spiritual man. I will be discussing with you how and when the devil chooses to attack you in your loneliness.

IN YOUR WEAKNESS

Jesus being tempted.

> Matt 4:1–11 Then Jesus was led by the Spirit into the wilderness to be tempted by the devil. 2 After fasting forty days and forty nights, he was hungry. 3 The tempter came to him and said, "If you are the Son of God, tell these stones to become bread." 4 Jesus answered, "It is written: 'Man shall not live on bread alone, but on every word that comes from the mouth

of God.'" 5 Then the devil took him to the holy city and had him stand on the highest point of the temple. 6 "If you are the Son of God," he said, "throw yourself down. For it is written: "'He will command his angels concerning you, and they will lift you up in their hands, so that you will not strike your foot against a stone.'" 7 Jesus answered him, "It is also written: 'Do not put the Lord your God to the test.'" 8 Again, the devil took him to a very high mountain and showed him all the kingdoms of the world and their splendor. 9 "All this I will give you," he said, "if you will bow down and worship me." 10 Jesus said to him, "Away from me, Satan! For it is written: 'Worship the Lord your God, and serve him only.'" 11 Then the devil left him, and angels came and attended him.

The Devil will attack when you're vulnerable, especially mentally and physically. Upon fasting for 40 days, Jesus was ambushed. According to the Bible. The Devil sought to physically assault Jesus at one of his lowest times. Not once or twice though, but three times. There are individuals who might just *cradle and safeguard their flaws*. You will never be freed if you are one of these individuals. I call them "The insecurity cradlers." The Devil has you in his clutches and will do all in his power to keep you there, cradling your problems, storing up your flaws and protecting your insecurities.

Insecurities are a weakness according to the devil. All he has to do is sow a little seed of doubt into your mind and he has you in his clutches. Thankfully, Jesus understands insecurity better than anyone. He acknowledges you're not flawless, but He also knows He can restore you. All wounds are healed by Jesus. Not by some connection or friendship, not through food or leisure, not through striving to please others, but through calling on the Name of Jesus.

Do you really believe the devil isn't going to try to tamper with you and your weakness? he tampered with Jesus, the true and living God. The King of Kings and Lord of Lord. He is obviously going to attack your little minds over any inconvenience. Have any of you watched Miraculous ladybug? I was so obsessed over that show, but my point is the villain (Hawk Moth) would've been keeping eyes on everyone just to see which one of them would've had an inconvenience that day and then would send out "aacomas" to them in order to get into their minds and control them. He was tampering with their minds and messing up their emotions to do seriously damaging things to hurt people and their families. Just so the evil (Hawk Moth) may seize control and wield power. Which is essentially what the devil desires. As a Christian, you must always cover yourself with Jesus' blood because it protects you, cleanses you white as snow and brings covering over every demonic influence.

THROUGH YOUR HEART

> Gen 4:2–8 Later she gave birth to his brother Abel. Now Abel kept flocks, and Cain worked the soil. 3 In the course of time Cain brought some of the fruits of the soil as an offering to the Lord. 4 And Abel also brought an offering—fat portions from some of the firstborn of his flock. The Lord looked with favor on Abel and his offering, 5 but on Cain and his offering he did not look with favor. So, Cain was very angry, and his face was downcast. 6 Then the Lord said to Cain, "Why are you angry? Why is your face downcast? 7 If you do what is right, will you not be accepted? But if you do not do what is right, sin is crouching at your door; it desires to have you, but you must rule over it." 8 Now Cain said to his brother Abel, "Let's go out to the field." [a] While they were in the field, Cain attacked his brother Abel and killed him.

On a more typical note, murdering your sibling is . . . excessive. It's also fair to be envious, given that the God of the Universe just turned down a gift. Why did God refuse Cain's gift though? Cain's gift was denied because of his filthy heart, not that it was made from the fruits of the field instead of a blood sacrifice. He may have brought his finest, but he did it with the wrong mindset entirely. This is equivalent to someone reluctantly donating a big

The Attack of Loneliness

quantity of money to the church. You see God looks at one's heart. Not forgetting He looks at your heart according to your deeds.

> Jer 17:10 "I the Lord search the heart and examine the mind, to reward each person according to their conduct, according to what their deeds deserve."

> Prov 4:23 Above all else, guard your heart, for everything you do flows from it.

> Matt 15:19 For out of the heart come evil thoughts—murder, adultery, sexual immorality, theft, false testimony, slander.

I hope you get the point; the heart is to blame for a lot of things. Cain's heart was not pure; it was filled with grief and jealousy, as well as wrath and iniquity. God forewarned Cain that sin was "at his doorstep," or that sin craved him. This serves as a reminder to us that sin in our life is always attempting to convince us to do deeds that disgrace God. This is pretty much what happened to Cain. Cain's offering, whatever it was, would not have satisfied God because of this. It was easy to form an alliance with sin when Cain hit a misfortune. He could have simply made it right instead of killing his brother. In this instance, do not succumb to loneliness's anguish and misery; sin will embrace you with open arms since that is what the devil desires. To curdle you in that lonely place. Instead, seek God and converse to Him; He is loving regardless of how you feel; he understands and is eager to assist and heal your deceitful heart.

IN YOUR PAIN AND MISFORTUNE

Whenever you're injured and in agony, the Devil will try to seduce you with fast remedies. He encourages you to think that he, not God, has all the answers. If you are experiencing difficulties in your relationships, he may nourish you with negative words and ideas about that person in order to further sever the bond. If you're sick or in misery, he'll attempt to convince you that God isn't present and doesn't understand what you're going through. If you do not follow God in these times, the Devil is evil enough to make you question if God is genuinely good.

One of my father's church members tragically lost their spouse to diabetes and their mother-in-law to covid. She also lost her mother a few months later. Isn't it terrifying? We hadn't heard from her in quite some time. Not in our services. There were no calls or texts. Her life appeared to be inert and lonely. She had a twelve-year-old son who experienced the same agony. I can imagine him not knowing what occurred or why it transpired. It turned out to be a sad catastrophe for her. Loneliness had taken over her life, and she covers her feelings better than anybody I've ever seen. Loneliness made an appearance and the demon noticed a route.

In life, there are two plans: the devil's plans and God's plan. It's whichever you give into. She lost hope. She lost her love. She lost her peace of mind. She lost her joy. Only God would have supplied that, no amount of words would've helped. The bottom line is God was waiting for her to talk. It was just up to her. It's up to you to speak to God on what you are going through. God is the supplier of all of your needs. He is your strong tower.

Questioning God, huh? I don't exactly recommend questioning God—it's not very healthy. It really just shows a lack of faith but let's be honest though, sometimes we do it without even realizing. Like "God, how could you allow him to break up with me just like that? Don't you want me to be happy? Get married? Have kids? Or God, how could you take my dad away from me? Why did you even allow that? I needed a dad and you took him away. I know it's difficult to understand the logic, but it's God's logic and God's Kingdom purpose. Years from now, when you have matured into the man or woman that God intended you to be, you will comprehend His rationale for your love life, and you may meet the perfect person with the right motives. One of the worst things to overthink is God's role in taking lives. We all have a time limit on earth. I want you to know that to be absent from this body is to be present with the Lord.

A pastor I know personally once said that God took his brother for one reason, because His brother was about to commit adultery with another woman. It would have caused a huge mess and God took him before anything could have happened. God took Him before he messed up his life, his family and another person's family. I know it's something to think about, God must have done that a lot to save peoples souls, but think about it that's how incredibly merciful God is, saving us from sin and Hell's consequences.

> Ps 46:1 God is our refuge and strength, an ever-present help in trouble.

> Ps 75:1 We praise you, God, we praise you, for your Name is near; people tell of your wonderful deeds.

IN YOUR TEMPTATION

Temptation is the impulse to indulge in quick pleasures that jeopardize long-term aspirations. Temptation also refers to the enticing or influencing of a person into doing such an act, whether by exploitation or otherwise of a person's interest, passion, or threat of losing something essential to them.

When we are lonely, we all feel the temptation mounting. Knowing this as a Christian is not rocket science, but it appears to be rocket science when you're alone and don't know how to go about it. Many of us are college students, and it is terrible to be away from your family, and it is tough to tell yourself that everything is okay. We fall short of the glory of God, and make no mistake, the devil sneaks in to keep you feeling lonely. Then there's despair, worry, overthinking, and guilt to contend with. If you are a member of Christ's body, you can be certain that the Devil will attempt to sabotage you. Although the Devil cannot be blamed for everything, there are many things that are the result of his work, and it is essential to note when he is at work in our own lives. He has the ability to ruin us and remove us from our Heavenly Father if we are not vigilant. Nothing could ever make him happier. However, when we are shielded and safeguarded, we have the ability to repel any of his strikes.

The theory of the fall is based on a biblical reading of Genesis 3. Initially, Adam and Eve lived in the Garden of Eden with God, but the snake persuaded them to eat the forbidden fruit from the Tree of Knowledge of Good and Evil (Read Genesis 3:1–24). The scriptures are plastered on the pages below as a reminder of the story in detail.

> Gen 3 Now the serpent was craftier than any of the wild animals the Lord God had made. He said to the woman, "Did God really say, 'You must not eat from any tree in the garden'?"

> Gen 3:2–3 The woman said to the serpent, "We may eat fruit from the trees in the garden, 3 but God did say, 'You must not eat fruit from the tree that is in the middle of the garden, and you must not touch it, or you will die.'

> Gen 3:4–5 "You will not certainly die," the serpent said to the woman. 5 "For God knows that when you eat from it your eyes will be opened, and you will be like God, knowing good and evil."

Instead of convincing Eve that eating the fruit isn't all that horrible, Satan whispered his way into convincing her that it will only bring you privileges and knowledge the same as God. The devil enjoys using this strategy to deceive people into believing that sin is gratifying and good. I recently saw a Tik Tok video with a doctor saying that masturbation is a beneficial way of producing sperm and can help prevent prostate cancer. We are all aware that this is a deception. Sin may appear and feel fabulous, but it is killing your spirit man and has repercussions if you do not accept it and repent.

> Gen 3:6–7 When the woman saw that the fruit of the tree was good for food and pleasing to the eye, and also desirable for gaining wisdom, she took some and ate it. She also gave some to her husband, who was with her, and he ate it. 7 Then the eyes of both of them were opened, and they realized they were naked; they

sewed fig leaves together and made coverings for themselves.

Gen 3:8–9 Then the man and his wife heard the sound of the Lord God as he was walking in the garden in the cool of the day, and they hid from the Lord God among the trees of the garden. 9 But the Lord God called to the man, "Where are you?"

Gen 3:10 He answered, "I heard you in the garden, and I was afraid because I was naked; so, I hid."

Since Adam and Eve were informed that eating that fruit was forbidden by God, you will see the repercussions as well as sin formally entering the planet. Take note of God's response after seeing them covered up...

Gen 3:11 And he said, "who told you that you were naked? Have you eaten from the tree that I commanded you not to eat from?"

Gen 3:12 The man said, "The woman you put here with me—she gave me some fruit from the tree, and I ate it."

Gen 3:13 Then the Lord God said to the woman, "What is this you have done? "The woman said, "The serpent deceived me, and I ate."

Gen 3:14 So the Lord God said to the serpent, "Because you have done this, "Cursed are you above all livestock and all wild animals! You will crawl on your belly and you will eat dust all the days of your life.

Freeze! Just so you know, serpents had legs back then. God is condemning the serpent to slither on its belly in this scene.

Gen 3:15 And I will put enmity between you and the woman, and between your offspring[a] and hers; he will crush your head, and you will strike his heel."

These are the penalties God imposed on women. Below, you will observe and comprehend why you experience discomfort when doing common womanly activities. Before you attack Eve, I'd want to emphasize with you that you also make bad decisions, and being spiteful is not the solution. God will not tolerate pettiness in Heaven or on Earth.

> Gen 3:16 To the woman he said, "I will make your pains in childbearing very severe; with painful labor you will give birth to children. Your desire will be for your husband, and he will rule over you."

Adam's punishment fell into this category; his penalty was now accepting responsibility for growing food for himself and Eve. He no longer had the capacity to communicate or cause trees to grow on their own, thus his punishment was work, followed by death, which brought sickness and old age.

> Gen 3:17 To Adam he said, "Because you listened to your wife and ate fruit from the tree about which I commanded you, 'You must not eat from it,' "Cursed is the ground because of you; through painful toil you will eat food from it all the days of your life.

> Gen 3:18 It will produce thorns and thistles for you, and you will eat the plants of the field.

> Gen 3:19 By the sweat of your brow you will eat your food until you return to the ground, since from it you were taken; for dust you are and to dust you will return."

> Gen 3:20 Adam named his wife Eve, because she would become the mother of all the living.

> Gen 3:21–24 The Lord God made garments of skin for Adam and his wife and clothed them. 22 And the Lord God said, "The man has now become like one of us, knowing good and evil. He must not be allowed to reach out his hand and take also from the tree of life and eat, and live forever." 23 So the Lord God banished him from the Garden of Eden to work the ground from which he had been taken. 24 After he drove the man out, he placed on the east side of the Garden of Eden

cherubim and a flaming sword flashing back and forth
to guard the way to the tree of life.

To be specific, a Cherubim is an angel sent by God to protect
the Tree of Life. The origin of the garden is yet unclear and under
research. Although, I think the Garden was swept away by the
flood caused by Noah and the ark, conspiracies remain.

I want you to focus on the portion where Eve succumbed to
the short-term temptation of eating the fruit, as well as the portion
where God chastised both of them, resulting in prolonged damage.
You see what happened is that Eve listened and gave into the temptation. The temptation was very short term, less than 5 second
bite and we can probably tell they both regretted it tremendously.
When God "caught" them in shame and figured what happened
He pretty much punished them *forever*. It did not end happily, we
can quickly say they cursed themselves and all humanity in itself,
it becomes easy to blame them but they're just like us believe it or
not. They were tempted and gave in. The difference is God did not
spare them. God basically cursed them, removed them from the
garden and cursed their marriage with enmity and their offspring,
tragic. As a result, the apple became a symbol for knowledge, immortality, temptation, the fall of man and sin. We shouldn't laugh,
though, since God has the freedom to withdraw from your life if
you go too far, because of Adam's sin men work like dogs, and
because of Eve's disobedience, women must go through several issues and extreme pains during pregnancy, but don't blame them
entirely since you're the precise reproduction of sin.

Short-term gratification for a long-term issue is closer to
nothing but the truth. They got agony, despair and *loneliness*
away from God and the garden, and so much dread, especially
in the Cain and Abel tale. You don't want God to abandon your
life and purpose; that's the absolute worst situation to be in, and
I wouldn't want that on anyone. Your continual disobedience and
failure to strive to avoid sin might lead to severe persecutions and
troubles in the future. Like watching porn for instance, let's say
you get married with your sin, *that's also very tragic*. It will mash
up and rip apart your marriage. Getting in a relationship with a

narcissistic girl just because she's pretty and marrying her because of outward appearance and sexual desires, *oh boy!!* Now that's a tragedy. I mean people can change with the help of God of course, but imagine marrying a woman with no Godly love or morals and she can't take care of a household, the complete opposite of proverbs 31. Honestly, you might be the most miserable and end up the loneliest man on earth because of this decision and I won't doubt if she became severely unfaithful to you and literally wrung you dry, so much so, you have less than $3 in your bank account. I rebuke that and I declare beautiful marriages and offspring's, with God's will off course. I'd suggest praying for your future spouses *right now.*

Before I end of this portion of topic, you may be asking me, well Rebecca will God disown me if I give into this sin. The answer is, No. He will never leave you. The only person He actually kicked and walked out on was Satan. Your sin will not prevent you from hearing from God. After Cain murdered Abel, God appeared to him before anybody else and said, "Hey Cain, where's your brother?" Not to add that God questioned him first, and he still lied and said he didn't know. Then God told him that He could hear Abel's blood pleading with Him. Guys, God is aware of your sins and temptations; don't act as though this is his first church session. Sin will not separate you if you own your errors, repent, and reform. Sin has the power to ruin your spiritual man, but it is up to you to stop it before it destroys you. I'm sure God is looking forward to hearing from you.

IN NEW SEASONS OF YOUR LIFE

Seasons and new chapters in life can be bewildering and depressing. As a Christian, you will experience different seasons: difficult ones, successful ones, beautiful ones, ugly ones, and even upside-down ones. That's okay; seasons serve the primary goal of educating, mending, and even providing joy. Loneliness has the potential to make you bolder, less fragile, and even spunkier. Most of us must have either slept through it or cooked or ate a bunch of crap during

Covid. That's fine; it's the same old story with me in 2020. We had a lot of freedom to just flourish during that dreadful season, but think if you spent time with God every day, worshiped every moment, mastered an instrument, or even published that book you'd been thinking about. It would have been fruitful, wouldn't it?

I suppose what I'm saying is don't squander your loneliness. There's something waiting for you there. It's your season. Perhaps this is a season when God is openly inviting you to join your church's worship team, to listen to Him in the silence and allow Him to speak to you, to attend Bible School, to build on your spiritual man, and to strengthen yourself. Open your eyes to fresh opportunities in Christ. God does not want you to stay where you are. He genuinely wishes to assist you in becoming the person He desires you to be.

By means of letting God speak through the silence, I do mean to sit in the quiet and rest in His presence a little. God actually has a lot to say. You may not fully understand God's humor but you will. Soon. If you stay connected to Him. In this new season or chapter, loneliness can take a huge toll on you . . . even when you sleep. Don't be blind to what God is doing to you during this time. You may be getting dreams of casting out demons, worshiping on a stage, ministering to people in Haiti or even seeing hidden sins in people's lives, a taste of spiritual discernment. I want you to know that when you enter the body of Christ, you are given a talent or you are anointed for a particular service. Rather, pray despite your loneliness, asking God to keep assisting and educating you.

Ishmael found a purpose in his season, regardless of the environment, regardless of how lonely he and his mother felt, and let's not forget that they had nothing in the wilderness. He just trained as an archer. Believe it or not, even through all that Ishmael's future was promising, far more so than you might imagine. Ishmael was promised by God that he would have his own powerful nation. And, believe it or not, he did.

One of my friends recently joined our worship team. He wanted to play the guitar. God literally blessed him with his own guitar, strap, case, amp and picks. The thing is the devil did not like the sight of this and decided to attack during this new chapter for him. He was attacked personally more than once, so much that he didn't want to play anymore. He decided that the devil can't win, and he won't. He set his eyes on one goal and that was to worship for God no matter how hard it gets. He took the bull by its horns, prayed and interceded because he knew that God is his strong tower no matter how disappointing and lonely this new chapter felt. At this moment, through trusting God he holds a lot of ministries. The persecution does not cease when you take up the mantle of ministry; in fact, it becomes much harsher and much lonelier the more you give to God. I know, the devil simply doesn't know when to give up or when to quit, how aggravating. Nonetheless, consider who your God is—prayer and reading the Word is what really empowers you. You need your spiritual fuel, Charles Spurgeon once said, "A well-marked Bible is the sign of a well-fed soul." And his words speak volumes. My last words to you on your new chapters, *never* give up and learn to rest in God's fulfilling presence. No matter how lonely it gets, God's definitely got your back.

IN YOUR EMOTIONS

The devil has a high reputation in targeting your emotions. Satan knows you better than you know yourself. Like the back of his hand. Every reaction. Every action. The way you walk. The way you talk and even the accents you use. How you sleep. Your most used words and phrases, the way you laugh and much more. He senses loneliness better than anything that is why when you feel alone. All of a sudden, depression kicks in, fear, overthinking, insecurities, insanity, suicidal thoughts and sexual immortality even. God tells us that He hasn't given us a spirit of fear but of love and of a sound mind, *God didn't lie* when He said that. Our flesh is incredibly fond of sin and its pleasures. It gives into every possible feeling. When you're stuffed on Thanksgiving but realize there's apple cinnamon pie and vanilla bean ice cream from Ben and Jerry's. So, you stuff yourself to the point where you think you're about to burst. That's essentially what your flesh does and how it responds to being overly stuffed by sin, and the devil wants you to *blow up*.

Some people experience loneliness as a feeling. It's normal. As previously indicated, social anguish draws in sin, and some events in our life may develop and create this psychological problem. What's the quick fix? Say no more . . . It's Jesus. I've been saying this like I've been singing the national anthem. *Talk to God* in your emotions. Simply converse to Him about those feelings. Sometimes, as a guy, you see this really sweet girl and you may tend to have feelings for her. Your body will send signals to you indicating a feeling of emotional or physical connection. You might lust after her when your alone, which are really ungodly thoughts. Instantly, as a Christian you should know, "Jesus, I come against every ungodly thought in my mind that's going to lead me astray and into sin, I rebuke every lie in my mind in the name of Jesus. Amen" it's that simple. God made it that *simple*.

If you have an eating disorder of any kind, let's just illustrate binge eating disorder. You wake up one day and you start your day healthy. As the day progresses you realize that you are getting the urge to binge or the urge to go buy the entirety of your grocery store and eat it. Rebuke that in the name of Jesus, right away. Jesus actually cares about your mental health difficulties. Massive or tiny. He is concerned and wishes for you to discuss it with Him. Don't be arrogant or haughty. He enjoys being addressed to and when you become honest with Him. He's that kind of God, amazing right?

> Gen 1:26 Then God said, "Let us make mankind in our image, in our likeness, so that they may rule over the fish in the sea and the birds in the sky, over the livestock and all the wild animals, and over all the creatures that move along the ground."

Emotions . . . feelings . . . mushy stuff . . . sensations . . . It's all fundamental of how God wired us, even Go has feelings, too, just like us.

He loves us.

> 1 John 4:8 Whoever does not love does not know God, because God is love.

> John 3:16 For God so loved the world that he gave his one and only Son, that whoever believes in him shall not perish but have eternal life.

I mean, obviously He's fond of us. Sending His only son to die on a cross to save you, me and everyone else whether it be Believers in Christ or non-believers. How good is that? I was actually speaking to a non-believer recently and she exclaimed, "How cowardly of a God to die on a 'cross' to save people. It makes no sense." Most of you reading this might be getting as angry as I was. Yes, I got really mad in that moment, there was no doubt about it. I knew she was mocking God, but instead of feeling angry, my spirit actually started grieving for her because I realized that she just rejected God just by saying that. I replied by saying, "Are you sure? Are you sure that's what you want to think? God really adores you, so much so, He chose to die on that cross. He was beaten, mocked, they dashed the crown of thorns on His head while He screeched out in pain to the Heavens. He used every aching part of His body, He summoned all of the breath He had in Him to ask God to show mercy to people like us. Are you sure?" she didn't respond. What really pains me is that people reject the greatest love in this world and I believe it's because they don't know that a greater love could exist.

Many can't comprehend how someone so merciful and compassionate could die for them, bearing disgrace and agony so that we may have a shot at Heaven. We never deserved what God did for us, and it's the reality that He lays His life on the line for us not once, but far too many times, just so you and I can be with Him someday. He is always thinking about you.

He has joy and actually laughs.

> Ps 37:12–13 The wicked plot against the righteous and
> gnash their teeth at them; 13 but the Lord laughs at
> the wicked, for he knows their day is coming.

God pretty much lives outside of time, so He knows the enemy is going to be decapitated and his reign is very short-lived. Hence why He laughs because the devil is already lost and can't be rationed with God and His power. The next time the devil comes in to plant seeds of doubt, tell Him to swallow those lies because God has a different plan and I am 100 percent sure God laughs at Him, all the time.

He gets sad and mourns.

> John 11:35 Jesus wept.

In this scripture, Jesus is well-aware He could've raised His friend Lazarus back from death to life but yet still, He wept for him. If you knew someone was suffering and on the verge of death but also knew they'd survive, would you cry and bury yourself in anguish? I'd guess not, but in the scripture, Jesus felt so much pain that He cried, even though Lazarus was going to survive. Why is that? We read before that God's love is greater and His love is higher than any other. This is a clear indication of God's love for us. It's so great that it's not understandable. That's some reckless love.

God feels pleased with us, especially when we pray and have small victories.

> 1 Kgs 3:10 And the speech pleased the Lord, that Solomon had asked this thing.

In this verse, God was pleased because Solomon asked Him for wisdom. He obviously gave Solomon wisdom and thereafter,

Solomon was also even given riches. Like I said, God looks at the heart and He knows that Solomon's heart was in the right place.

God rejoices in victory.

> Ps 104:31 The glory of the Lord shall endure forever; the Lord shall rejoice in His works.

You are His work. Please don't forget that, He created you and had every thought of forming your nose or body the way it is. He rejoices when we speak to Him. He rejoices when a soul gives their life to Him. He rejoices when we overcome temptation. Never take these things lightly, God is really proud of you. You are entirely His miracle.

He becomes displeased sometimes.

> Num 11:1 Now the people complained about their hardships in the hearing of the Lord, and when he heard them, his anger was aroused. Then fire from the Lord burned among them and consumed some of the outskirts of the camp.

Picture being a Youth Pastor, and you see a kid of yours smoking. How would you feel knowing you teach your youths against these things? Displeased right? Not angry but just displeased and disappointed. God feels that too, especially if we whine for little things, it shows zero faithfulness and it infects other people too.

He gets angry.

> Exod 4:14 Then the Lord's anger burned against Moses and he said, "What about your brother, Aaron the Levite? I know he can speak well. He is already on his way to meet you, and he will be glad to see you.

> Num 14:18 'The Lord is slow to anger, abounding in love and forgiving sin and rebellion. Yet he does not

leave the guilty unpunished; he punishes the children for the sin of the parents to the third and fourth generation.'

Don't get scared. He's only angry for a moment. God isn't very fast to anger like we are but He gets angry over injustices like rape and murder. He gets angry over selfishness and greed. He gets angry over sin. That's why we have repentance, it may not sound like enough to God but it is and it will please Him. With that being said, God does not hate you or have resentment against you because you fall short, He hates your sin. Even the disciples sinned, it might've annoyed Jesus for a couple seconds but He knew the big role those disciples were going to play in His story. He never resented them, He instead befriended them. It's the same with us, even though He angers over our sin, He still wants a relationship with us because He knows our calling and He knows the amazing purpose He has planned especially for you.

God is full of compassion.

Matt 14:14 When Jesus landed and saw a large crowd, he had compassion on them and healed their sick.

The bizarre thing is that we feel compassion but not as much as God. See, we feel these things a lot of the time, but trust me, God feels them a lot more. When God urges us to donate our clothing to the impoverished or to prepare a wonderful home-cooked meal for the destitute, we become oblivious to it. Many of us may feel called to be missionaries, but you're not listening to God. God gave us this passion and desire to do the same to Jesus, so that we might be like Him or at least educate you concerning Him. When a person is explaining their misfortunes to you it isn't only ethical of you to love and pray for the person, but it is also important to help them. Even if it's a dollar to buy themselves a happy meal.

God is jealous sometimes.

> Exod 34:14 Do not worship any other god, for the Lord, whose name is Jealous, is a jealous God.

Some of us may be in a relationship or have friendships, right? How do you feel when your companion shares a relationship with another? Jealous right? God becomes jealous when we put things in front of Him, like our phones or social media, maybe a boyfriend or girlfriend or maybe even your job and money. These things are "distractions." Our schedule should be built around God, not whenever you get time.

God hates . . . but only 2% of the time.

> Prov 6:16–19 There are six things the Lord hates, seven that are detestable to him: 17 haughty eyes, a lying tongue, hands that shed innocent blood, 18 a heart that devises wicked schemes, feet that are quick to rush into evil, 19 a false witness who pours out lies and a person who stirs up conflict in the community.

God hates the sin, not the sinner. God hates your sin, *not* you. So, if you were created by God and in His image, then that means you have His characteristics . . . not just physically but emotionally. God invented emotion. He basically gave it to us so we won't be walking around like zombies and robots. We can have feelings and love Him in return. It can be a blessing and a curse, I know, but God has His reasons and it's totally valid. You're probably wondering, again, "What's this got to do with loneliness?" Well, you see, our emotions, especially when you feel them strongly . . . makes you feel alone or caught up inside your head.

Let me make it simple, when you're sad do others feel exactly what you feel? No, to some lengths they don't. When you're angry at your parents and they don't understand you . . . you feel alone. When you point out an issue or a dream you're compassionate about and everyone laughs at your thoughts, you'll feel lonely because no one understands you. When you feel hate for something someone did and everyone else is pretty normal with it, like if you see the school bullies torturing a 12-year-old, you might sense the pain and loneliness of the person and it becomes worse when nothing is done over the matter.

When you fall in love, not everyone understands, people may have rejections to your type. Especially, when hormones kick in and you want feel or touch. Parents are not understanding here, *sarcastic laughs*, but God does because sexual desires is also something He wired you with. When you feel complete displeasure with someone or something like your grades and you don't know how to get better at math or physics, loneliness kicks in, school isn't a walk in the park, it gets lonely.

As a human, you might comprehend something to a certain level, you can guarantee that God understands it to a far greater level—the greatest degree there is. Talk to Him about your feelings, no matter how crappy they are. Pray about it; I'm sure God will appreciate hearing from you. Simply pray, "God, assist me with my emotions, give me self-control." It won't happen overnight, but give it time and allow God to enlighten you.

CHAPTER 5

Hidden in the Lonely

Loneliness is hidden.

❉

A BOY WITH A BAD PAST

I have a tale of a very good friend of mine, from whom I obtained permission to write this section of my book. For reasons of privacy, I shall not reveal his name. Simply refer to him instead Adam. Adam was the family's firstborn. I assumed they were always a good family, but it turns out Jesus had only recently entered their life. Moving on, when he was younger, his parents didn't spend much time with him, which caused him to feel neglected and hurt. At such a young age, he was humiliated and mistreated for a variety of unforeseen causes in his parents' lives. When he was three, his dad abused him and threw him outside to grieve. His mother was equally terrified of his father. Adam didn't understand, but every night when he thought about what was happening to him, he'd cry and lay down on the concrete outside their house. He had no idea that this demon known as loneliness was coursing through his life like a bullet, penetrating every nook and causing him misery. Thank God for his grandparents and aunt, who largely took good care of him. Despite this, he lived for many years with an orphan spirit.

For those of you who are unaware of what an orphan spirit is, it's basically a spirit that corrupts your mind and tells you unhealthy things like: "You are not loved and no one likes you." Or "No one wants to be your friend and no one will ever want to hang out with you."

Years and years passed and Adam had a love interest. She was quite the enthusiast, very radiant and God-fearing. He knew what he felt for her, but because of his past which involved unhealed hurt, it almost broke them both. Ironically, she was a daughter of God and had Christ-like, loving and stable parents. She grew up with confidence and with a joyous spirit. There was by no means she came into this man's life without reason. She was a warrior for God and so none of her prayers for this man went into vain. He healed. He also became God-fearing. It was only because of God and her request to Him for this man, the spirit of loneliness, anger and depression in his life actually left. He used every piece of resilience he had because—*he wanted to heal, he didn't curdle his flaws and demons.* Adam also knew that if he wanted the girl, some serious change was going to have to take place. He knew that in order to reach her, he had to reach out to God first.

Even though I am 18, I always tell people, even when I preach, to heal and prepare before you have kids so that they don't go through the same things and worse than you did. I preached on this sermon called, *"Raising a Secular Generation"* and really the purpose was to reach out to the parents and kids on raising a generation who can fight and be Christ-like because most of the time parents are the ones who hold back their kids, they're the ones who devalue God's word and they're the real distractions in a child's life: making school, activities, materials and a career more important than God and church. Church has a big role to play in a child's life as well, it is vital, church prepares the food you need for the week. *Your flesh is weak, spiritual food is needed.* Do not isolate yourself from God and church, *that's just worse.*

> Prov 18:1 Whoever isolates himself seeks his own desire; he breaks out against all sound judgment.

For such little youngsters, the spirit or demon of loneliness can strike the kid if the parents, because of whatever circumstances, don't really invest enough time with the kids! Whenever this occurs, the demon of loneliness haunts the little boy or girl! Putting an orphan spirit into their lives which they will take into their later life and relationships and even marriages if it isn't fixed.

AN EFFORTLESSLY LOUD STEREOTYPE

It was only lately that I had this encounter, and it was all about my title. "Pastor's daughter" is a label that occasionally hurts my joints. In my situation, these preconceptions imply a great deal of guilt and insecurity. Many kids and others may look up to me or claim they do, and I always respond, "I really shouldn't be your role model; Jesus should be." Mostly because He's flawless, and in my eyes, I'm not. People literally ignored me because of it several times, which hurt. I'm not a biter. They have the impression that I am severe and uncool, or that I am too devout (which I find nothing wrong with), but I constantly assure them that I am very down to earth, and I am. People just do not take the time to recognize it. Paul claimed that in order to win the Jews, you must be exactly like them . . . however, it doesn't apply for me . . . tragically. It truly became a nuisance, and I kept worrying that something was wrong with me. I wanted to understand that the light that radiates within me and God's face shining upon me meant a lot towards certain individuals.

Teens today share my desire for healthy, Godly, trustworthy, wise, and polite companions. Hey, I know the Bible says loneliness is bad and that being in your thoughts may make you insane. But hear me out: God will always be your best friend, and that will never change. He sees your emptiness, He watches over your tender hearts, and He will always love you. He is the embodiment of the ideal buddy. You may believe that you must be this cool guy who blends in with the crowd, but my friends, when you walk with Jesus, you will always be an outcast. To fit in, you don't have to be wicked, disobedient, use "cool" vulgar language, have sex, lie, or take drugs. It is not required with God. Jesus was never one to blend in. People had to blend in with Him. According to the Bible:

> Jas 4:4 You adulterous people, don't you know that friendship with the world means enmity against God? Therefore, anyone who chooses to be a friend of the world becomes an enemy of God.

> Prov 22:24–25 Do not make friends with a hot-tempered person, do not associate with one easily angered, 25 or you may learn their ways and get yourself ensnared.

You don't want to be unfriended by God and entangled with the wrong people, so please reconsider and alter your decision; godless and immature friends generate enough havoc to turn your entire family against you, your school, and God. When you are alone, the demon of loneliness may have more motivation to take over your life. Surround yourself with His splendor on a daily basis. Get some food and watch a Christian movie. Make little dates with God. Yes! You must have heard me. Dates. Dive into God's infinite and never-ending love and anointing. Jesus is and always will be your best buddy.

I'm going to embarrass myself for a moment and show you this poem I wrote five years back for a drama monologue, when I was really struggling a lot:

> "Yeah, I'm the Pastor's Kid. What a ludicrous stereotype. Yeah I may be physically beautiful to you, spiritually stable to you, emotionally stable and I have it all together, to you.
>
> Nobody saw me on a Sunday morning looking at every flaw in my body. It took me 20 minutes to get ready but the other 50 minutes staring at myself in the mirror because I just wasn't satisfied. In my eyes I was so deformed, ugly, lazy and obzocky. I wouldn't want to look anyone in the eye because I was afraid of them realizing how ugly I really was. Cover up my insecurities. Afraid to take a picture because I'm insecure and extremely revolting.

No one saw when I struggled so much with my walk with God. When I wouldn't even look at my Bible. When I wouldn't even say goodnight to God far less for a good morning. I listened to ungodly music and hoped I felt better with crying spells. I'm not even sure if I'm going to make it to Heaven anymore since I've failed so much.

Fraudulence was another fear.

No one saw when I was lonely, crying just for a hug from God, the anxiety attacks in the depressive episodes inside of my room. When a dark room felt better and when the lights were on it was weird and bothering. When I shared a laugh or smile—deep down all I wanted was to explode.

It may look like I have it all together but really, it's all hiding behind my stupid little stereotype. God, I need you to refine these flaws of mine. Please, I need You more than anything."

And, funnily enough, I got a B—on this, the point is I really struggled at the time and I still suffer from time to time. This walk isn't perfect for me, either. I'm not that different from anybody else. I'm not sure why people demand such a thing as perfection. Perfection becomes very lonely. Obligation is lonely. Expectation is lonely. If only someone could come out and just say it. What I really can say, that is encouraging for anyone or any pastor's kid reading this is . . . *God is your best friend since humans aren't sure of themselves.* The nights where it's just you and God. You and your Bible. Maybe, some tears were falling but that's okay because I'm pretty sure He's teaching you something, especially how to rely solely on Him. *God wants you to Himself.* Bear in mind that He is a jealous God who will go to any length for you. He knew how you felt and what you were going to say or think when you cried out to Him. Nonetheless, He hears and comforts you. How incredibly respectful and kind is that? He's incredible. I just discovered that God is the only thing a human being requires when there is an emptiness within them. Jesus is the perfect remedy.

Jas 2:23 And the scripture was fulfilled that says, "Abraham believed God, and it was credited to him as righteousness, "and he was called God's friend.

Prov 18:24 One who has unreliable friends soon comes to ruin, but there is a friend who sticks closer than a brother.

John 15:15 I no longer call you servants, because a servant does not know his master's business. Instead, I have called you friends, for everything that I learned from my Father I have made known to you.

A PASTORAL LIFE

Let's hear it for my mom and dad, Whoop!!! Whoop!!! Give it up for the guy who helped shape me into this great and Christ-centered human being; just a moment to thank him and her for being so terrific. My mother is also a pastor, but she is incredibly eloquent and humble in all she does—so much so that she does not rush into high-ranking roles like preaching and worshiping, or anything else that involves being in the spotlight. She's more of a caretaker or hardworking backline worker for our ministry—I know, very humble—but she also doesn't approach people with her position, which I like. She is our backbone.

I certainly know that being a spiritual leader is really difficult. As I already stated, loneliness creates space for several other things. You don't have many friends as a man or woman of God. It's the loneliest profession imaginable. I've watched these two blessed individuals go above and beyond for their people, praying for them and providing for them, and they're outstanding at what they do. What I've found is that they suffer spiritually in forming relationships, there is a lot of envy, anger, and a lot of expectations—so much so that there is fear of losing their self-image, which I always try to explain is uncontrolled, especially since the devil knows it's a weakness. As a result, folks typically aim for dragging their identities through the mud. For this reason, one of the many things I've always promised myself is that I'll never marry or become a pastor.

God, on the other hand, most likely has different ideas but for me it's just too much.

I believe though, that it is a high-ranking title to own and for that many people pretty much hate you. Especially, people who sink themselves deep into witchcraft, law of attraction and manifestations. That's because the devil does not want them or any spiritual leader in fact to spread the gospel. We all know Satan is sulking over the fact that the gospel is being preached everywhere and he's losing this battle.

Being who they are, isn't pretty. It's actually very mentally, physically, emotionally and spiritually draining to go through, every-single-day. A little advice, pray for your pastors, they are going through more spiritual warfare than you might know off. Loneliness is something they go through and I know that for sure because they miss each other dearly whenever one of them leaves to do their job. Also having a daughter, I know they feel bad for leaving me alone at home sometimes and even for days at a time. To be quite honest, sometimes my parents don't even see me and I don't see them. It gets lonely, sometimes we don't even understand each other's own problems (like every other family) and even if we are in the same situation . . . It still seems very lonely.

I remember when I was younger, living in an old boarded house. My mum had left her job and just started staying home to take care of me and my dad worked two jobs. There was a desire in their hearts for many things and one of them was to have a nice home. So, they started breaking ground and guess what, they had no money. They started our home with seven thousand dollars, which was not their money, it was actually mine given by my grandpa. They fought through to the very end to be at the place they are today, a nice home, their own church and food on the table. No one saw the struggle, the tears, the long lonely nights and a troubled spirit tugging at their hearts for my future. Down to this very moment, people give jealous glances, spread rumors and splatter their names like it's their business, yet they have no idea the blood, sweat and tears that went in so that they could be the people they are today.

We went to another church twelve years ago, before they became pastors. Like any church, they were kind of toxic and harmful in some ways but it was because my father had recently begun preaching and the leader of the house disliked him for it. No judgement—at some point every single person experience jealousy. People enjoyed the way he related to them while preaching since he was the youngest and finest at what he did. Many other preachers admired him for it. Many congregations wanted him to come over and preach at their church, but his pastor didn't like it. To cut a long tale short, the Pastor would constantly preach against my parents casting shade at them on a Sunday morning in front of everyone in the congregation. Unfortunately, my father never had a true father figure in his childhood, which left him with a significant burden. My grandfather died before I was born, so when he went to that church, he wanted to look up and see this man of God as a spiritual father. This did not occur; instead, this pastor decided to envy them both.

Nonetheless, God appointed them to be pastors, which is a big responsibility, but the enemy never stops striking. I know they have felt lonely in numerous circumstances where others have been disgusting and cruel to them. They learned to create a wall in front of them for safety over time. That is just how every human reacts to pain. They create barriers, and so do I. They adore people . . . and some from very huge distances, haha! Your pastors are also humans. Any pastor reading this would agree that they are not bots. They, like you, are flawed and might sometimes fall under the expectations of God's word.

Just like you, the issues they've faced could have done two things to them—make them braver and tougher or weaken and smash them and their faith in God into pieces. Those two are exceptionally strong people and I commend them for being such inspiring examples for both the youth and young at heart. They never allowed anything to shake their faiths or stop their lights from shining. They always trusted God. No matter when they lost hope, strength and feelings of losing their dignity. They can proudly say, God pulled them through every situation.

JESUS' LONELINESS WASN'T UNDERSTANDABLE TO THE HUMAN MIND

I openly told you these stories above because loneliness exists even among those with strong callings and titles. People who have a lot of friends, I'm sure, feel lonely as well. Jesus was popular, yet he was also lonely. They celebrated Him the first week and crucified Him the second. It wasn't all rainbows and colors for Him either. Jesus, the Messiah, God's Son, King of Kings, Lord of Lords . . . was also alone. So, my question to you is, "What makes you think that loneliness would not enter your life and keep you alone?" because it can, and that demon is unconcerned with who you are, what you do, or what your calling is.

> According to society, within modern culture, isolation is a secret people maintain – frequently even from yourself. Loneliness carries a negative connotation. There seems to be a common misconception that if you're lonely, it's your entire fault, *false.*

Now ask yourself this question, "was it Jesus' fault for being lonely while He was on earth? And you might just think . . . *no* . . . it wasn't. You're perfectly correct, it wasn't Jesus' fault. His father was in Heaven, many people could not understand Jesus sometimes either. Let me draw an example: do you guys remember when Mary came to Jesus during this wedding celebration and she said, "We are out of wine." then Jesus replied saying, "Woman! It is not my time..." and Mary was probably so confused but the thing is, Jesus' language versus our language is different. Jesus' thoughts were probably like this wine is equal to the shedding of blood, which means Jesus thought she said, "Give me blood." or "I want your blood to shed." cool right? So, for those of you thinking: "I wish I could just sit and talk to Jesus." trust me, that might be a little hilarious.

Let's simmer down a bit though and talk about Jesus, did you know that Jesus, like us—has needs too? When you pray, do you listen to what God has to say? Probably not, because you like when God listens to you. That's why you don't understand what God is doing sometimes, because you're not listening, neither are you paying any attention. Yes, we praise God, every second of everyday I sing and worship to God. Whether I'm washing the dishes or cleaning, doing my assignments, I am praising God, but Jesus' needs are far more than just a sound or shout of praise, He needs you to listen too.

It was difficult for Jesus when He was on earth. For many people, one-way communication gets tedious; how do you feel when someone is discussing something as uninteresting as carpentry? Bored, right? God, too, requires your attention. Is that correct? Consider how many times God has prepared to speak to you just to have you chat to Him about that new vehicle you've been eyeing and then depart for another distraction. How do you feel when others completely disregard your suggestions? Precisely. You walk into that atmosphere of praise, worship and intense anointing and then leave God in that place, *alone*. Without letting Him give input. Imagine God like, "Thank you my child, that was amazing, I hope you feel much better now that I dried your tears. I want you to know I love you but before you leave . . . please wait, don't go just yet. . ." and then you leave. Think about how often you do that? Probably all of the time.

He wants to tell you what's bothering Him too. Maybe the relationship that you are involving yourself in was never His exact intention, maybe He wants to teach a little bit more, maybe He is trying to tell you there's still so much I have planned for you, yet still, we don't listen—*heartbreaking.*

Here is a story of Jesus and the disciples, and how Jesus actually responded them after the disciples did not recognize Him. They were heartbroken by the death of their Lord. They did not recognize Him in their anguish. To truly grasp our Lord's great need, pay close attention to Him as He walked beside those discussing, mourning disciples. They were conversing and debating with one another.

> Luke 24:13–27 Now that same day two of them were going to a village called Emmaus, about seven miles from Jerusalem. 14 They were talking with each other

about everything that had happened. 15 As they talked and discussed these things with each other, Jesus
himself came up and walked along with them; 16 but
they were kept from recognizing him. 17 He asked
them, "What are you discussing together as you walk
along?" They stood still; their faces downcast. 18 One
of them, named Cleopas, asked him, "Are you the only
one visiting Jerusalem who does not know the things
that have happened there in these days?" 19 "What
things?" he asked. "About Jesus of Nazareth," they replied. "He was a prophet, powerful in word and deed
before God and all the people. 20 The chief priests
and our rulers handed him over to be sentenced to
death, and they crucified him; 21 but we had hoped
that he was the one who was going to redeem Israel.
And what is more, it is the third day since all this took
place. 22 In addition, some of our women amazed
us. They went to the tomb early this morning 23 but
didn't find his body. They came and told us that they
had seen a vision of angels, who said he was alive. 24
Then some of our companions went to the tomb and
found it just as the women had said, but they did not
see Jesus."

What a lonely man Jesus must have been. He wanted to speak
to them since he had so much to say to them. And when He could
no longer keep quiet, Jesus quit listening and began to speak.

Luke 24:25–27 He said to them, "How foolish you are,
and how slow to believe all that the prophets have
spoken! 26 Did not the Messiah have to suffer these
things and then enter his glory?" 27 And beginning
with Moses and all the Prophets, he explained to
them what was said in all the Scriptures concerning
himself.

This was one of the only times Jesus experienced a two-way
conversation, between Himself and the disciples.

Luke 24:30–32 When he was at the table with them,
he took bread, gave thanks, broke it and began to give
it to them. 31 Then their eyes were opened and they

recognized him, and he disappeared from their sight.
32 They asked each other, "Were not our hearts burning within us while he talked with us on the road and
opened the Scriptures to us?"

The scripture above is what they said after Jesus left. They
said, their hearts burned. In this story I can imagine Jesus feeling
a sense of fulfillment because He got to speak and they listened. It
wasn't about their joy alone or even your joy as a disciple of God.
What about God's Joy? We discussed that God has joy, right? But
how often does He feel fulfilled? Like Elijah, the great prophet, we
are more familiar with demonstrations of power than we are of
His still small voice. He also has a need to speak to us. Listen. Although, I envision a risen Lord, tears running down His glorified
face, strolling down that dusty road with a joyous heart. He had
been satisfied; his desire had been answered. While the world waited, Jesus paused the entire salvation plan for a few hours —simply
to converse! I picture Jesus beaming. He'd served as a minister. He
had had His first two-way communion in His exalted form. He
had poured His heart out. Someone had touched his lonely heart.
His need had also been satisfied.

I don't know if it's just me, but do you guys remember when
your teachers would say, "fingers on your lips and listen up?" we
need to learn to listen to Him more often, it'll save us from trouble and also leave God feeling fulfilled instead of alone with His
thoughts on things that concern you. It's a win-win really, all you
have to do is listen. Did you know there will be a day where God's
heart won't be lonely anymore?

Rev 21:3–6 And I heard a loud voice from the throne
saying, "Look! God's dwelling place is now among
the people, and he will dwell with them. They will be
his people, and God himself will be with them and be
their God. 4 'He will wipe every tear from their eyes.
There will be no more death or mourning or crying or
pain, for the old order of things has passed away."5
He who was seated on the throne said, "I am making
everything new!" Then he said, "Write this down, for

these words are trustworthy and true." 6 He said to me: "It is done. I am the Alpha and the Omega, the Beginning and the End. To the thirsty I will give water without cost from the spring of the water of life.

This means there will be no division between us and God one day, face to face, in Heaven and the Lord's heart will be full of joy and fulfillment, talking to us.

CHAPTER 6

The Demon of Loneliness

The spiritual attack of loneliness.

✳

I thought God couldn't help.

When someone hears the word demon, they immediately think of sin since sin is something demons torture or tempt us to do. Loneliness is not a sin, although it is associated with a demon. People may believe that as Christians, we have it all together or that we are always cheerful and have no troubles . . . respectively, no, because:

> Jas 1:2–4 Consider it pure joy, my brothers and sisters, whenever you face trials of many kinds, 3 because you know that the testing of your faith produces perseverance. 4 Let perseverance finish its work so that you may be mature and complete, not lacking anything.

> 1 Pet 5:10 And the God of all grace, who called you to his eternal glory in Christ, after you have suffered a little while, will himself restore you and make you strong, firm and steadfast.

> 2 Tim 3:12 In fact, everyone who wants to live a godly life in Christ Jesus will be persecuted,

1 Pet 4:19 So then, those who suffer according to God's will should commit themselves to their faithful Creator and continue to do good.

There're also many more verses where that came from but as Christians, we will always have trials. Most of the apostles besides John had a gruesome death. John died of natural causes while the rest of them suffered persecution. John was at Jesus' side all the time and up to the very last, John wrote the book of Revelation and then he died. Just a fact, but as a Christian please expect the devil to tempt you continuously. Different day, different battle. That's okay though because the Word says that trials make us stronger and braver. Loneliness is a part of it.

This demon called loneliness will come at that time in your life when all of your ungodly friends walk out on you and say things like: "you're good for nothing and nobody likes you, you should just die. Look at you, ugly. You're a fraud. You sound funny or you walk funny. You're the reason people stay away from you. Your parents must be so embarrassed." *Total lies.* What those demons feed off of is when you believe the lies. Don't believe it. Plug in those headphones and blast Reckless Love if you have too. Jesus loves you. He created you the way you are. Makeup won't get rid of the insecurity. Makeup and tiny clothes won't make you confident for long. Being quarterback on your team isn't going to make you any less lonely either. Getting strong, muscular and drinking protein powder isn't fixing you. The only person who is able to crown you with that confidence is Jesus. Stop giving the enemy room for lies and deception.

As Christians we need to learn warfare. What we see with our natural eye is nothing compared to the spiritual realm. The spiritual realm is more real than the things we see nakedly. In fact, if a Christian cannot decipher or discern demons or heaviness in places that have demons—they are called *blind.*

The spiritual realm there are wars taking place. Regardless of our viewpoints, a struggle is raging. We are either winners or losers. Jesus had come and triumphed, already, so even if you think you faltered or failed, that's very okay. In the heavens, the battle has already been won. The spiritual realm is very real, more real than what we see. Don't be like a 3-year-old who plays peek-a-boo and thinks no one can see her when she closes her eyes and gets caught. This fight isn't for the physically strong but spiritually strong. In the spirit realm demons are targeting you, looking for an angle to shoot their arrows of loneliness, depression, bondage, anxiety, insecurity, shame and much more deadlier things that can kill a spiritual man. Never to fear though because God is here to protect you. He sends His angels specifically to protect and watch over you, angels don't miss, they're well-trained.

You might ask, well if the spiritual realm is real and the devil is shooting these arrows of loneliness at me or this demon of loneliness is constantly bugging me, what should I do? Well . . . I thought you'd never ask:

- Rely on God's power
- Prayer is essential
- Worship is Key
- God loves Unity
- Remember who your God is

RELY ON GOD'S POWER

> Isa 41:13 For I am the Lord your God who takes hold of your right hand and says to you, Do not fear; I will help you.

Did I mention that God is perfect, already? He is. He is also the perfect helper in times of need. Most of us reading this book have been struggling in some way or the other. I'd just like to ask, "Did you ever ask anyone for help?" besides God. How did they respond? Most of us do things as a result of a cry for help . . . but no one notices do they? There is someone I know who does. His name is Jesus. You probably saw that coming.

You can rely on Him at any given time. I know that many of you day by day, watch yourselves fall apart over life. Don't do that,

Jesus wants to help you. You see, since God created you, He will try to mirror Jesus' life on earth unto yours, meaning that He'll try to confront you with the very same problems Jesus faced. Why do you think your life is so troubled? Why do you think God allows you to feel the way you do sometimes? Because it's how you grow. He tills your soil, and it might pain you but the reason for that is because He wants to bring forth new soil into your life. In order to succeed you have to allow your King to help you, that sounds weird to say since human Kings don't actually help personally, but this King does. He wears a Victor's Crown and He overcomes.

PRAYER IS ESSENTIAL

> Rom 12:12 Give me relief from my distress; have mercy on me and hear my prayer.

> Jas 5:16 Therefore confess your sins to each other and pray for each other so that you may be healed. The prayer of a righteous person is powerful and effective.

Prayer is something all of us should be doing, whether it's morning, noon and night. Even Jesus prayed. At the front of this book, I quoted a scripture saying that even Jesus withdrew from the lonely places and prayed. Sometimes, you need extra reinforcements, the battle for your soul is bigger than the wars happening on earth. Even Satan doesn't want to be alone in Hell, *so he's rooting for your soul to burn with him.* Hell is full of Pastors who are well-known, full of Kings, Queens and Politicians that served well on earth and even the biggest millionaires and tycoons on earth who were all led astray by the devil.

Not to worry the God of all the Heaven's hears you and sees you and is also rooting for your soul to be in paradise with Him. We may not be able to pray for hours but make sure to never go an hour without praying. The devil is waiting for a slip to catch you just like in Miraculous ladybug. Hawkmoth was waiting for someone to break in, in order to capture them with his Acoma's. That is why spiritual body-building is essential in this Christian walk. The devil wants to keep you in this constant bondage. Let Him know that Jesus lives inside of you and in your home and there is no way loneliness is going to get to me today. Claim it today, by the blood of Jesus that this demon will not seclude or isolate me.

WORSHIP IS KEY

> Jer 20:13. Sing to the Lord! Give praise to the Lord! He rescues the life of the needy from the hands of the wicked.

Worship and praise. Where are my worshippers at? Yes, scream out Jesus' name with a song. Get into that atmosphere of praise and worship. Just lock in and glorify Jesus for a bit. You may be folding the laundry, washing dishes or vacuuming. Praise God! Worship Him! Exalt Him! Don't go a second without Him. He is your strong tower, your fortress. His word says that the weapon may be formed but it will not prosper. Worship Him every day, not just on Christmas or Sunday mornings. Being lukewarm isn't a nice place to be in. Loneliness can surround you like smoke, don't give that devil room.

GOD LOVES UNITY

Two hands are better than one. How good does it feel to find out you weren't the only person to forget doing your homework? Gives you a sense of comfort, right? Like phew, it isn't just me. This is the purpose of unity, to stand together. I am not saying don't do your homework, be obedient . . . ha-ha!!!

You all will be surprised to find out how much God loves unity. Unity and fellowship are very important to God. I said unity because talking to someone or talking to a mentor or pastor will make things much easier. Talk it over some McDonald's, some steak and truffle fries or maybe coffee. Mentors are there for you for this reason. Spiritually, sometimes we need a mentor to direct us. Notice I did not say friends because some of us lack in that area, like me. Mentors can be your youth pastor, your pastor or an older person you trust. Let them know the spiritual battles you are facing, they'll direct you. *The older will teach the younger.* They have gone through and are still going through battles as well. Trust their advice. They may be old but they are bright and are full of wisdom.

Once you learn from the older people, you'll have a clear idea of what to do. They may tell you to fast and pray for a week, listen to their advice. Something may not work as quick and some demons in loneliness need an extra shove down the pit of hell but I promise you all things pass away. It might seem like this devil won't give up but He isn't mightier than Jesus. Jesus will reach down to you or meet you where you are struggling most. Just continue praying and worshiping and don't stop asking your mentors and elders questions, they have a lot to say and teach.

REMEMBER WHO YOUR GOD IS

The enemy comes to steal your joy and replace it with isolation, he comes to kill your peace and give you death and he comes to destroy your life and mess you up. Very recently in my country of Trinidad and Tobago, 5 deep sea divers were heading down the ocean to fix a pipeline that was broken. While fixing it someone turned the pipe on and it sucked all five of them inside. Let me just say, God knows what He's doing and when He's doing it. One of them was Christian and very ironically, he was the only one to survive because the rest suffered air-deprivation and critical injuries, so they were unable to crawl out of the pipe before they died. However, the man who was Christian turned around and told his fellow brothers, "Please don't be scared, Jesus is our savior, believe and He will save you." and with that he crawled out for help, but no one got there in time and the coast guards prohibited anyone from entering the waters. That man saved all 4 men that day, who could have died from eternal fires. Many people will not understand but God knew what He was doing.

That battle must have been hard for that man who survived. He may be questioning God with so many unanswered things.

He's probably so lonely in his thoughts, isolated from everything because he just doesn't understand. That demon found room to enter his life but what he doesn't realize is that he won 4 souls for the kingdom. Again, this battle is not for the weak, it's not for the fastest but for those who endure right until the very end. God knew why he took them so early in life, he knew why one person survived to tell that story and save them and He knew why it happened the way it did entirely.

No matter what happens, do not give up. Endure to the very end. Spiritual battles will increase. Loneliness will come from time to time to seclude you with your thoughts and emotions. Don't let that devil win. His destiny is to lose. Remind him that his time is up. Jesus won a long time ago. The devil might have had a plan in those pipelines but God saw it and changed the route entirely. Understand how big God is. Loneliness and seclusion are dead to Him and it will be for you too. Just *endure* and remember that God's thoughts and plans are greater than ours. He sets plans in place we may never understand.

> Gen 4:7 If you do what is right, will you not be accepted? But if you do not do what is right, sin is crouching at your door; it desires to have you, but you must rule over it."

CHAPTER 7

A Little Church Hurt

Have you experienced church hurt?

✳

I wanted to be forgotten.

You may wonder how loneliness is related to the church. As previously said, I am a pastor's child, and I see the church through a unique set of eyes. It's unfortunate that this isn't spoken more frequently, but church hurt is real. I've heard more negative than positive rumors about me. I've noticed comments that have startled even me. I can tell this with certainty: *church isn't perfect.* You may believe so, and the moment you begin visiting a church, the church becomes faulty, since the church is filled with imperfect people. That is why there are so many church hoppers. Every church has challenges, both visible and invisible. Being a pastor's kid puts me right in the center of everything, and loneliness in church becomes all too real for me. Aside from how amazing the service is always, I always feel seen—yet unnoticed, and I mean this in the greatest manner imaginable. People at church assume they know who I am, but they don't. I'm always clinging to my mom like glue, mostly because of people, their attitudes, trauma from previous occurrences with church members and even leaders, and trust troubles.

In the past, persons that I was close to from church who I thought were my friends, actually weren't genuine. They'd spread lies, twist my words and spread rumors that just aren't true. I have some serious fear when it comes to speaking face to face with people. If you ask me to preach or worship, totally fine. Face to face just isn't an option. Church hurt can be difficult and not being able to find a church where people actually spread love instead of hate, rumors and glances, can seem lonely and impossible, sometimes. We all long for Christian friends and the right church family. I personally wrote a few instances here on when I felt loneliest involving church activities and how Jesus was always the One, *I chose never to fail,* instead of people. It really just describes how I felt and how I expressed it through Jesus.

I explained before how I felt worshiping in the past and how unfortunately rude and unsupportive some people can be when you're trying to do God's work. It's not easy when people are breathing down your neck. Yes, they're probably around you, but that doesn't make me feel any type of comfort because I know half of these people either have something against me or aren't genuine. They have heard rumors and believed them, watched me with so much hate and tried to dig faults into my life. I know some of you might relate, maybe if you go to school, you'll know that rumors spread like wildfire.

Ever heard the term, "watch your step." Yes, sometimes you have to watch your step. At any given moment, Satan can use someone or something to distract you in the worst possible way or spread a rumor about you just because they don't like you, especially in churches. My best advice is to *love them,* but from an *exuberantly* huge distance. My mum told me, "Who's for you, is yours. You may not see it through people at first or even after you're close to them because friendship is blind, true friendship is when someone or some people truly love you and have your back, even behind your back."

The Church is not for criticizing people. You go to church to worship God and listen to the Man of God's sermon. Fellowship is important, but don't judge people or immediately just not like them because *"you feel"* like they're not good people. Never ever judge people, big or small, no matter the portfolio they hold or not. It's not your job or place.

Young people, especially one's like me see fault in even the greatest congregations, young Christians who don't have a solid foundation would see this as hypocrisy, that is why we need proper church leaders and mentors who can properly address these things.

I distinctly remember times where we'd have occasions at church and we had to fellowship together. Fellowship amongst church members is a rare and beautiful thing, I can't lie. Although, during these times I'd feel eyes, glaring right at me, laughing and I knew I was the problem because I'd hear my name calling a lot. Phrases like, "what is she doing?" or "what is she wearing." Maybe comments like, "she probably has dreams of her Bible at night." Or "she thinks she's all that because she's a pk." And I tend not to make things worse, I try to act like everything's okay but sometimes it's way too much for me. I usually start shivering around certain people or start crying, whichever occurs first. The anxiety becomes real at church. For years I have been dealing with this and honestly it doesn't get better. I always have to think about what people will say, judge me by or find fault in. Which isn't healthy because the only person you should be trying to make proud is God.

For instance, there's this other time, an usher at a church literally became aggressive towards a young woman because of the way she dressed, I remember her dressing in this pair of white jeans and a long-sleeved sweater. I asked myself, "well . . . What's wrong with her outfit?" To me, there was no problem, it was modest and it also was her first time at the church. I know that if you guys go to the mall, you'd wear something quite similar. Even if there were rules for dress code, it was her first time and obviously, she was clueless. I get that you need to have respect for God, but God is always with us. I got to figure out the girl had limited outfits and couldn't afford it at the time. This honestly made me so upset. After a year, I visited another church (not the one she went too first) and this beauty had an anointing to worship. She was glowing. She really let God's light shine through her, regardless of the church hurt she received. Now imagine, if that usher had been nicer to her? She would've taken membership at that church and been a worship leader there, right? But instead of showing people love and compassion, we show them rudeness and hate. Her leaving the church could've been avoided and she could've been a great blessing to the first church. *God never makes mistakes, though.* As far as I know, we are trying to win people, we are trying to mirror Jesus, I don't believe people call themselves Christians for doing this. Yes, I believe that modesty is important, like when someone's wardrobe has a serious malfunction for instance, but if a new-comer comes to your church and they wear pants or they don't have proper church attire, would you tell them to go back home? No, the Bible clearly says, *"Come as you are to Christ."*

Don't get me wrong, these things also happen in reverse. Pastors are occasionally erroneous in their teachings and may be rude and dictatorial. Some are simply interested in the benefits of ministry which does a lot of harm to their members. People also harm other people in church, forcing them to leave. Some people do harm to others while also acting as victims of the situation; I refer to them as Jezebels or Jezzy's. A lot of spirits lurk in churches today, the devil loves to cause division amongst church members and the only way to get rid of it is through the help of the Holy Spirit intervening. And don't get me wrong I totally understand how church and ministry is inherently traumatizing to many. People are unhealed from these things, which makes them problematic sometimes because their church trauma crosses over into their ministry.

One of them in particular came to my house unexpectedly, to blame both me and my mum for spreading rumors about her and her children, but because of privacy reasons, the identity of those people will not be revealed. When in reality, she spoke to everyone about her business, with her own mouth. Those were lies, she dug the hole too deep for herself and she was also trying to get my dad to side with her. Obviously, my dad read right through her and knew she was lying. Thank God for discernment, which pretty much allows him to see the good, the bad and the demonic, but she eventually left our church with the excuse that "her kids and herself were uncomfortable." Sad to say, I believe this person believes their own lies too. People never fail to surprise me anymore. One of the things I did was build a wall around people who has caused hurt to my parents and I. Which isn't the best idea, although I know people can be hurtful, it's always best to show the love of God instead.

I still struggle with uncertainty and fear to this day. I did realize, though, that the only person who truly counts is God and His plan. Through all of the ups and downs of my painful past. The lies and dishonesty from those that attempted to undermine my family and I, I've truly matured, and not only that, but I've grown to use my solitude and confinement to accomplish better in my alone time. Developing the abilities and gifts that God has given me. One of them being stealthily writing this book.

When I saw someone from church, I'd joyfully smile and say, "hiya, how are you?" And I won't receive a response—just pride and ignorance, and to be honest, I've also learnt to be a better person. I learnt to ask myself what Jesus would do or say in similar situations—He would turn the other cheek, be courteous, keep His head up since He is God's Son and show His never-ending love. Trust me, if your church hurt, your feelings are very valid. The best thing you can do is take it to God, He's got the best advice and knows the best way to comfort and validate someone, but . . . the real question is, *did Jesus receive any similar church hurt or ministry hurt?* Yes, He did from His disciple, Peter. Peter was a former fisherman, whom Jesus promoted to "the fisher of men." During his ministry with Jesus, Peter actually denied knowing Him, leaving Jesus feeling betrayed and lonely. Stating the obvious though, Jesus still never cast Peter aside, He just asked Peter three times if he truly loved Him. Imagine that!

In fact, lots of people hurt Jesus. They rejoiced with Him the first week and then by the second week, they nailed Him to the cross, spat on Him and beat Him to death. They mocked Him, they asked Him, "where's your God. now." You know what Jesus said after all that massive hurt and rejection, "Father, forgive them, they don't know what they're doing." Jesus is my actual role model in Christ. I won't deny it. I'm not perfect and neither are you. If you have suffered from church hurt, admire how Jesus dealt with it. Admire how He responded and mirror yourself the way He did. It's going to hurt, but I assure you it'll teach you many things.

It is normal to fail. It is fine to make errors. Don't ever allow church hurt to cause you to knock down your mantle. If you worship, worship for God to grow in anointing and talent. Do you enjoy ministering? Put your trust in God and His word. Use your alone time to attend Bible School. If you want to be an intercessor, PRAY! PRAY! PRAY! Improve your abilities. You will not be disappointed if God helps you reach for the stars for the sake of His Kingdom. Do it for Him, and you *will* be successful in whatever you endeavor. Put Him *first*, and I guarantee you that blessings will pour in like never before.

If it's one thing I know for sure, church hurt disturbs both parties of an issue. It isn't easy for either side. Both sides undertake faults and flaws. The one thing I know will *always* fix church hurt is confrontation, which the devil hates because he does not want people working in unity, which I will talk more about. Here are some steps in resolving church hurt:

- Pray!!!
- Confrontation is Key
- Forgive! Forgive! Forgive!
- Allow God to heal you
- Show love

PRAY!!!

Remember that church isn't perfect and people are not good at love. Pray for them, just like Jesus did. Church hurt is difficult so please, go to the one who is love and talk to Him. Prayer softens our hearts as we let go of those people. Learn to rest in His presence. Jesus told us specifically in:

> Matt 5:43–44 "You have heard that it was said, 'Love
> your neighbor and hate your enemy.' 44 But I tell you,
> love your enemies and pray for those who persecute
> you.

He did not imply we should like or disregard them, but rather that we present them before God's throne and bless them with our devotion. Sometimes, you never know the trauma a person has gone through before, make sure to calm down and pray before you lash out with anger and hurt them even more. Put Jesus in the middle of every situation. Let's refer to David from the Bible, he was so God fearing—even when he was angry, he told God and even when he wanted to kill those three men, he told God. God never allowed him to murder but even in those times of aggravation he prayed.

CONFRONTATION IS KEY

> Matt 18:15 "If your brother or sister sins, go and con-
> front them with their fault, just between the two of
> you. If they listen to you, you have won them over.

A scriptural meaning of confrontation is having a face-to-face interaction with someone in order to apply God's word to a problem. This must be done with humility and with love for God and the individual being addressed. We are to communicate the truth in love in order to praise God and help the individual.

Confrontation is never easy. The devil absolutely despises confrontation and the reason for this is because after confrontation, comes forgiveness and unity. It doesn't matter what the issue is, confront the people that hurt you, in doing so the situation can settle without exploding or going too far. Everyone has faults and everyone makes silly mistakes. You also are going to hurt people at some point, the important thing is that the issue becomes resolved and the persons involved are left undisturbed with their feelings validated. This also stops individuals from feeling lonely and isolated in the problem, having no one to understand.

You may not know this but the Holy Spirit is so sensitive that it knows when there's tension and when there's tension, the Holy Spirit can't move as it pleases too. That tension between both parties of a situation will hinder the Holy Spirit from moving and even speaking as it should. That's how important confrontation is. Confrontation can save a lot of relationships and friendships.

Confrontation is unavoidable in life. Others will confront us if we have harmed them or if they sense we have made a mistake. When other people offend or harm us, we will confront them, which is healthy as long as our reasons are correct. It is unacceptable to use confrontation to humiliate, criticize, or exact revenge on another person. God declares Himself to be the avenger, and He reserves the right to punish wrongdoers accordingly.

Avoiding conflict may appear to be a desirable thing, but there are instances when it is required, and avoiding it is incorrect. If Jesus had not openly confronted the Jewish authorities, their dishonesty and oppressive methods would have persisted. If Paul had not faced Peter, Christianity may have deviated into legalism or a version of Judaism in the first century. If Nathan had declined to approach David when the Lord sent him, David may not have been restored to relationship with God, and Israel would have perished. We'd also lose out on some of the classic psalms, such as Psalm 51, David's cry of repentance.

Refusal to engage in confrontation may provide individuals with momentary peace, but it may come at the price of the other person's well-being. We don't hesitate to alert someone who is heading toward a drop-off zone. We may even have to question his belief that the road is perfectly safe. But we know better, and knowing what we know is in his best interests. As Christians, we know something that the rest of the world should know. Some people may reject our approach. When we call sin by its proper name, some people feel furious and protective. However, Christians are required to reject misinformation and preach the gospel, even if it feels hostile to the listeners. When the confrontation is done with love and humility, it may do a huge amount of good.

FORGIVE! FORGIVE! FORGIVE!

This has got to be the hardest thing a Christian could ever do, especially after facing so much hurt. Unforgiveness could land you a seat in Hell. I am saying this in the best possible way, *forgive every single day.* You don't know how much time you have left on earth and the day you close your eyes and God asks you, "Why didn't you forgive your brother?" or "How could I forgive you after hurting Me so much?" listen God isn't blind to your hurt, He knows. You need to come to the conclusion that God is forgiving and you should be too. People are not perfect. Neither are you. Be forgiving and do it with humility.

If you're stuck in a place where you're having trouble forgiving your friends, your parents or even church members, God is the best teacher. He's also the best forgiver. Before he died on the cross, He asked God to forgive the people that crucified Him, and imagine He did that smack in the middle of His death. Make it known to God that you desire to have a forgiving heart and He will guide you.

> Matt 6:15 But if you do not forgive others their sins, your Father will not forgive your sins.

ALLOW GOD TO HEAL YOU

"Healing is the children's bread." Remember when I explained that wine translates to blood? Well, bread translated to Jesus being a healer, He is the bread of life. Jesus suffered for your healing and now healing belongs to you. Healing is a strong part of growing. Again, it has the potential to make or break you. Allow God to restore you, and you will develop and evolve in your life and Christian walk, but remember to forgive the people who hurt you, first.

SHOW LOVE

Show the love of God. They may expect you to lash out, but *what would Jesus do*? Jesus would've turned the other cheek like He did in the Bible. Pray for them, give them a smile, saying 'good morning' to them as usual. You don't have to be buddies again but you can love them......................................*from a distance.*

CHAPTER 8

Why God?

Why does God put us through loneliness?

✳

G od has never once done something that was out of line or proportion, *He is perfection.*

1 Corinthians 14:40 But all things should be done decently and in order.

What I mean is that God would never let you toss away something that was not part of His plan, certainly if you are faithful to Him. In this section. I want you to know that God never makes mistakes. Your loneliness was not an accident, and as you read this chapter, you will have a deeper understanding of the subject. Some of the sub-topics being described are:

- He is seeking your attention and time, on Him alone
- To speak to other lonely people
- Removing ungodly habits from your life
- Prepare you for ministry and leadership

HE IS SEEKING YOUR ATTENTION AND TIME, ON HIM ALONE

> Eph 6:18 And pray in the Spirit on all occasions with all kinds of prayers and requests. With this in mind, be alert and always keep on praying for all the Lord's people.

God is pleading with you to get to know Him. This is not like other beliefs where we need to say prayers and sing hymnals like the national anthem, we get to be *personal* with God. Meaning that, us, as humans get to speak to the true and living God. Who is loving and kind in all His ways. We don't have to complicate things, light candles, go to a special room or even do any kind of action. We just have to open our hearts, lock in and talk to Him, whenever and wherever. Cool, right? Because He loves us so much that He is allowing us to be personal. Anywhere, at any time and with any circumstance. He is seeking to spend time with you during your loneliness. He *wants* to be with you.

Have you ever seen a romance movie, where the guy chases the girl and continues to pursue her no matter what, with every flaw and imperfection. Yet, he still continues to run after what he wants. That's basically God but with a lot more passion and love for us. He leaves the 99 to come find us, when we are lost and can't find our way back. You need to understand that you are like a rose in God's hands, precious in His eyes. You hold value to Him. He just wants your time. God should be your schedule, everything else must circle around that. And don't forget that it is a *two-way* conversation, you have to make the extra effort to hear Him out as well.

TO SPEAK TO OTHER LONELY PEOPLE

> Jer 1:8–9 Do not be afraid of them, for I am with you and will rescue you," declares the Lord.9 Then the Lord reached out his hand and touched my mouth and said to me, "I have put My words in your mouth.

I know it seems insane, but talking to other lonely people? Your loneliness educates you. It teaches you how to lean solely on God. It trains you to be self-sufficient. It teaches you how to fight spiritual battles. It instructs you on how to speak with God. When you can converse with God, He will pour out His entire being on you. One of them is an anointing to love others like He does. When He achieves this, it will become extremely easy for Him to communicate with others. It makes no difference whether you are educated or not. My father preaches to individuals who have large enterprises and PhDs, despite the fact that he is not as educated as they are. Why is he addressing brilliant thinkers right now? Because he was called to it. He is called to preach and counsel, and I believe it is because He spent His lonely time communing with God.

And don't worry about not understanding what to say or how to talk; God will put the perfect words in your lips at the right moment, just as He did with Moses, who had a speech impairment; if Moses can do it, so can you. Allow the Holy Spirit to guide your words. Everything you do, whether you walk, talk, sing, or dance, must be for the glory of God.

> Matt 10:19 But when they arrest you, do not worry about what to say or how to say it. At that time you will be given what to say.

REMOVING UNGODLY HABITS FROM YOUR LIFE

> 1 John 1:9 If we confess our sins, he is faithful and just and will forgive us our sins and purify us from all unrighteousness.

> Gal 5:16 So I say, walk by the Spirit, and you will not gratify the desires of the flesh.

Believe it or not, when you are in your lonely places it can be very easy or very difficult to get rid of your ungodly habits. It depends on how you spend your loneliness. Are you scrolling through Tik Tok or are you reading your Bible? Although, if you're suffering with masturbation or pornography or any other ungodly habitual sin, this one's for you.

Rethink how you utilize your time. Make a list of all the things you need *to do* and under that make a list of all the things you need to *fix*. Finish up all the things you have to do: homework, make lunch, go to the grocery with your mum, do the dishes at dinner, spend time with God and even finish up on that series you've been trying to finish up on. Make sure that everything is done. Now move on to your "fixing list." I know some of you need to fix your sleeping and eating schedule, go to bed early and have some dinner. If sin is on your list to be fixed, pray about it. Don't stop there, do it every single day after that. You start off day 1-5 mins of prayer and reading one chapter from your Bible. And then increase every day by 5 minutes.

I am aware the Bible can be tough to understand, though I recommend watching videos on YouTube that can give you a depiction on the stories and a showdown on the drama with modern English. Old English can sometimes really be difficult to interpret. At this moment, you can thank God for technology, so now you can better understand His word through the use of YouTube and other apps.

PREPARE YOU FOR MINISTRY AND LEADERSHIP

> Gal 6:9 Let us not become weary in doing good, for at the proper time we will reap a harvest if we do not give up.

During my lonely times, those were the moments God was really preparing me for greatness. I really can't tell you how grateful I am that I was given that lonely season because without it I'd be exactly where I was before it. I remember those really painful days where I'd walk the halls of my classes and auditoriums in school and I'd think: *what's wrong with me?* Or why do I feel so alone here? why can't I fit in with any clique at all? But it was all this time God was using those lonely moments to help me understand that He does not want me to be like them. *He wants my life to mirror what He wants it to be.* It was a hard transition, God tilling my soil was a hard transition but that is okay because it prepared me for my ministerial duties and leadership.

Where you want to be may not be where God is calling you, and where you absolutely would rather not be could be where God is calling you. It prepared me to relate to individuals and youngsters my age who are dealing with the same issues I am and the world's problems. By reading His word, He sharpened my ax to communicate His word fluently. Wisdom and insight began to emerge at that point. The issue was that I did not want to see it. My attention was elsewhere, on making friends and obtaining popularity. That is most likely not God's intention for your life, and it is undoubtedly far larger.

God is attempting to instill courage in His children. He wants you to stay on the battlefield and not surrender. Stop begging God to remove your loneliness and issues and instead ask Him to arm you. Ask Him for the assistance and recruits you require to win. Even if you lose, God has already won the victory for you. He desires that you fight the good fight.

CHAPTER 9

"Wait!! Just Embrace the Lonely."

Waiting during the lonely and letting

your lonely cause a shine

※

Waiting in the midst of loneliness? Waiting for the perfect opportunity to embrace loneliness? Accepting something voluntarily while doing it enthusiastically or wholeheartedly is what it means to embrace. The question is; *How can you passionately embrace your loneliness?*

I don't imply go find a boyfriend, start partying, or start doing drugs because you're lonely. If you rush into a relationship to early and think your embracing your lonely, politely that is incorrect. Rushing into things before God gives an 'okay' can make a big fat mess and cause a lot of hurt. Partying is not embracing neither does drugs, those things only carry you further from God, have bad effects and horrible influences in your life.

What I meant was that when you're lonely, just be *productive* with yourselves. Be happy. Make the right decision to spend that time with God. Express yourself completely. Join your local worship team. Participate in a Bible school. Take that time and devote it to God. Keep smiling, even though it is difficult when you feel so alone, but smile. God is the only person who can shift those sad, lonely moments and put that grin on your face. He's a delight in itself. He brings you joy in the morning and evening. In difficult times, he is your source of comfort. I know how difficult it is to be cheerful when all you want to do is pout on Tik Tok or YouTube and tell yourself, "I don't like people anyway." Or "I'll be lonely forever." Learn to be productive. Make certain that your loneliness is alleviated and rest in God's presence.

Some of you may be in this lonely waiting period; like waiting to be accepted by your dream University. Some of you all are probably waiting for your dream job to contact you and some, like myself, are probably waiting for a publisher to recognize and publish their work. Let me be real, your *"no's."* your *"wait and be patient."* or your *"I regret to inform you..."* they're all just doors shutting in your face but make no mistake, God is providing a door for you. Don't throw away your waiting period being lonely and sulking when Jesus is driving you down the lane of success. *Celebrate* in your lonely, while you await that, *"yes."* It may not be what you want, but trust Him. Everything will work in His favor. What more could you possibly ask for then God writing your success story? Shift your focus on the one who is able to *shift* the situation.

Spend that time with God. God is looking at you in your loneliness, on your bed, with no socks on and chips next to you while you waste hours on Tik Tok thinking that it's going to help you when He knows that it's not. Social media, sleep, overeating and even medicine doesn't even cure your mental health. It just suppresses it. People say there is no cure to feeling lonely or feeling mentally ill but there is. The answer to your loneliness is Jesus. And don't even think about how you're destroying your calling because you've been wallowing in loneliness recently. Darlings, you are not powerful enough to wreck your destinies. The mantle is still over you; pursue it as you pursue Jesus.

I'm not trying to be weird but I've read the book of Esther 17 times in total. Yes, I counted. You might be like, "Rebecca . . . but why?" To be quite honest, I can read that book over and over in my spare time and still love it. I love reading it when I feel secluded in my thoughts. God's word brings so much comfort to me, that story with Esther is like a comfort story to me. I recommend finding a book you really cling too from the Bible and read it. It's okay to read it 100 times. God just wants you to occupy your time doing something for Him. Besides that, you can always talk to Him. Tell Him what you feel or cry out reckless love in your shower. It doesn't matter. Jesus is your healer in your loneliness. Express that feeling unto God and I'll assure you, there is comfort like no other with God.

5 things to embrace loneliness:

- Redefine Loneliness
- Give your loneliness Opportunities
- Your wingmen
- One day at a time
- Celebrate!!!

REDEFINE LONELINESS

Before we start high school in my country, we take the SEA examination. This exam is taken in order to get admitted to the best secondary school possible based on our grading scheme. I knew from an early age that I had the ability to go into a pretty good school because of how devoted my parents were to supporting me with things like additional lessons and classes. I scored an incredible 95.35 percent overall and finished in the top 100 in my country. Unfortunately, I did not get into the school of my choice. I got into one of the most despised schools in my country. Mistake? Maybe.

What I did not understand was that God was teaching me something really important through that lonely period. I was only thirteen at the time, I saw everyone passing for their first choices, to some of the best schools and here it is . . . I got the lowest ranking school possible. I felt disappointed in myself. My head flustered. I felt lonely. I felt secluded. I questioned God. My parents decided that this was a mistake and things needed to change. They knew something was just off and weren't about to give up on me. During that time, I had to wait. I had to seek God's hand unto my future and life. The period was so sickening that I just cried every day, I felt depressed but I waited on God in hopes for a response.

My parents applied for a transfer the next week after results and by God's Grace, two schools accepted in God's favor. The school I absolutely was hoping to attend, rejected me after hearing my dad was a pastor. The school was not Christian-based and said that they will not allow any Christian students to transfer into their school. The principal rejected the transfer thereafter, leaving me even more secluded in my thoughts. The second school was actually my first choice, which the principal quickly accepted and I spent the next 5 years there. Which, by the way, was the best 5 years ever. Five most teachable years of my life. In all honesty, I never thought I'd get to attend a prestigious school. I never thought the principal would've accepted my transfer request either since the grades to get in were so competitive. It never crossed my mind that I'd stand a chance of acceptance at that school but that thought me one very important thing, only God can qualify you. Not even your grades and own hard work and sacrifice. Nothing happens by chance. Even when you flip coins for a coin toss, God is in control of that.

After that period in my life, I decided to redefine my lonely situations and think of it as God working on it. The loneliness at that time would have turned into depression. In fact, in every aspect of my life, it could've turned into severe depression. God alone knows how I ended up being such a bubbly child regardless of everything that tried to tear me down. Even after being bullied for years and years. It's also the fact that every time I try to open a chapter in my life there are always stumbling blocks, obstacle courses and lengthy waiting periods, even seasons of hurt and disappointment in the middle of all that. God continuously molded me and it's only because *I allowed it*. I didn't allow the negative past and other occurrences to define my life. I redefined the way things were happening and reassured myself that even though this life can get disappointing and solitary, God will continuously lead me, taking me to every destination I needed to be in and at the right times. Don't define your life as lonely, redefine the loneliness in your life.

> Rom 8:28 "And we know that in all things God works for the good of those who love him, who have been called according to his purpose."

This verse demonstrates clearly that your life is following the path of God's purpose, and that no matter what you try to do or what occurs, He is inevitably in charge.

GIVE YOUR LONELINESS OPPORTUNITIES.

Think of loneliness as extra time on your hands. I know that loneliness can seclude you so much that you feel like you can't move from your bed. Listen, *get off your bed!!!* and do something. Achieve something. Create something. Add something great to your life. I know that that's so hard. I know, trust me I do. Loneliness can make you feel so unloved, so unappreciated and so demotivating but listen, you won't regret giving yourself opportunities during this time. Create an online Bible study and invite people at your school, spread the gospel of Jesus Christ. Take your little brother or sister out to get hotdogs. Join your church's intercessory nights. Join your local church's worship team. Play an instrument. Preach in front of your mirror or take the night off and do a little self-care with some good podcast.

I been repeating that so much but my point is; you never know what these little things can do for you and how far you can reach with it. Honestly, I thought none of those things would've helped me but it did. I'm now a worshipper, a young minister, soon to be author and a degree graduate, I'm not sure what else God has planned for me but I do know that you guys are the ones to make the first step of destroying loneliness and replacing that time with something good. You have to make the first move. You can't expect God to come into your room and drag you to youth group, you have to do it yourself. Then He will do the rest.

If you're lonely thoughts are making you question if God sees you and if it really makes sense, it does. I thought for years that even God didn't notice me, but He did. A long time ago, a prophet came to our church and she said to me, "I'm going to sing the heart of God to you, this is Him speaking don't ignore Him!" and God was literally *singing back to me*. He spoke to me in the language I always speak to Him in, through song. He even called me Beloved which is a name I continuously addressed God with. I'd always speak to Him with the name "Beloved" and for me that was so awesome because that just meant God was listening to me and looking after me this whole time. He sang back to me saying the sweetest things and it was such a special moment for me at that time since I really believed that God was ignoring me. I'm saying all this to say this, your special in the eyes of God, He notices the language you use to address Him and He sees you. You just have to give Him that room to also speak to you and respond to you in your loneliness. Don't shut out God because you think He's not here for you. He will *never* leave neither forsake you. Give Him the *opportunity* to speak to you in your quiet times, don't just speak, *listen*.

YOUR WINGMEN.

Some of you guys may know what a best friend feels like. Let me tell you about these three Guys who will always have your back. The Holy Spirit, Jesus Christ and God.

> John 14:26 But the Advocate, the Holy Spirit, whom the Father will send in my name, will teach you all things and will remind you of everything I have said to you.

The Holy Spirit is your teacher. The best teacher you will ever have. He is your wingman. You like the girl but she isn't for you, He is the perfect person to tell you, "Louis, that girl ain't the one God has planned for you. I think that it is better to wait. You know the Bible says to guard your heart. Bad idea man." And with all love the Holy Spirit will watch you ignore what He says then watch you come right back to Him because you know *He was right.* He is like your best friend. No human is going to come close to His dedication towards your life.

> John 14:6 Jesus answered, "I am the way and the truth and the life. No one comes to the Father except through me.

Who's Jesus, though? Some believe He was simply a wonderful teacher or prophet. Others claim that he was a decent man who performed good things. Some say He was a liar or a madman and those people simply just don't understand. And millions of people have worshiped Him as their risen Lord and Savior throughout history. Whatever your thoughts are on Him, I'm sure you'd agree that He stands alone at the heart of human existence. Jesus is Lord. But out of the Three in One situation, Jesus is basically the humorous One. Obviously, Jesus is rooting for you. He is the only chance you have to Heaven and He knows that. Which is why He wants to save your soul and be at the center of your loneliness.

> 2 Cor 6:18 "I will be a Father to you, and you will be my sons and daughters, says the Lord Almighty."

> Ps 103:13: As a father has compassion on his children, so the Lord has compassion on those who fear him;

God is basically the Dad of the wingman group. He's protective and authoritative. He knows how to set a record straight while doing it in a tender way. He may be a little slow while you're waiting in loneliness since His timing is different. A thousand years for us, is a day for Him. Even if there's no results right now, it's coming. Focus on God by the time. That time you have does not need to be consumed on episodes of depression or overthinking. It can be productive, your answer of course, is to trust that your Father knows your heart and knows your situation to bring you out of it. A lil faith won't hurt. It can go a long way.

Embracing your loneliness won't be easy. It won't be an overnight success story. I guarantee that when you put your trust and issues in Christ, He is more than able to heal, protect and pave the right future for you. And don't go trying to keep things to yourself. God, Jesus and the Holy Spirit is your main support, that's what they're here for. Allow them to consume your lonely thoughts and situations.

ONE DAY AT A TIME.

I just know that you guys have a fair idea of what *"wait"* means and an accurate idea of what it feels like to wait. Waiting is one of the worst things, especially if you're hungry. The tension builds and you may get crankier as the minutes pass by.

I also remember a time period where I was waiting to be accepted at a University. Took a while, I eventually gave up, thinking they just rejected me or threw aside my application. So, I sent in an application to KFC and Starbucks. They did not accept my CV to work for them, long story short. But eventually, I did get in, a week before actually. In my dream school and program where I feel so comfortable in, knowing that God was the one who opened that door. Take a wild guess at how I know that? I filled out the wrong University application and sent it in. Somehow, strangely . . . I got in. Listen, if it's for you, I guarantee you it's yours and if not, trust God. God is your final admittance. On a side note, I can testify that the stories I tell you in this book are the least strange things that has ever happened to me.

I can also testify that every time I tried to do something in my life, contrary to the devil's plans, which includes this book you are reading . . . something always went wrong. I always felt so lonely, when in reality God was planning that chapter for me with every ounce of His goodness. *Take it a day at a time*, listen to God, wait on His decision and I promise you . . . there will be no disappointment.

CELEBRATE!!!

> Ps 20:5 May we shout for joy over your victory and lift up our banners in the name of our God. May the Lord grant all your requests.

> Ps 126:3 The Lord has done great things for us, and we are filled with joy.

As humans we celebrate everything. We celebrate birthdays, anniversaries and even world dog's day. It's all just a celebration. Christmas is the world's biggest celebration which is the birth of Jesus Christ. But have any of you ever felt lonely on Christmas or lonely on something as a birthday? Have you ever cried on your birthday? Have any of you ever felt lonely during a family trip or maybe at your church?

I know that most of you might've answered that question with a yes, it'll be so cliche if I said, "you know what that's okay." because it isn't. That's a pretty messed up feeling. Seeing that I am a pastor's kid, there were times when there were Christmas dinners at our church for certain ministries which I was a part of and wasn't even asked to participate. It's almost like I was invisible. Growing up, I'd always asked myself, "girl, what is wrong with you?" because I'd get treated like that by people close to me as well. Uninvited. Neglected. Unwanted. It's not a nice feeling when everyone is gathered around fellowshipping and there I am—alone and once again, shoved aside.

I am not the only person in this world that feels like this and the devil might trick you into thinking that you're the most hated, most unwanted person to exist and that's simply not true. God is trying to invite you to celebrate with Him. whether it be through worship or praise or prayer. He wants you to know that there's so much joy in Him waiting for you. As Christians we are commanded to give thanks in everything. Paul said this in *1 Thessalonians 5:18-19: "Give thanks in all circumstances, for this is God's will for you in Christ.* In every circumstance, celebrate!!! Because with whatever your feeling God is doing great things.

Whenever you feel secluded in a room full of people, don't pick up your phone in front of everyone. Get up or create a conversation with someone, anyone at all. Make a new friend at school. Sit next to new people from other classes. Now, there's no guaranteed expectation that everyone will come to love you. Some people won't like you just because you are you and there's God's light shining over you. I will tell you this, there's no "liking process" or "falling in love process" with God. He loves every inch of you since the day you were conceived and has not stopped to this day. Unlike people, God doesn't have to spend time with you to love you or even ask you to be perfect in order to love you, *He just does*, and knowing that should be a comfort, but don't be afraid to make some friends and form conversations first; things can change.

When Paul, for instance, was locked up in jail and sitting in the dark, decided well, hey, maybe I should get up and do something for once instead of sitting around in this sad, lonely jail cell. He asks Timothy for his books and starts writing and spending time with God and get this, he wrote most of the New Testament in prison. Amazing! I know some of you are like, well that's not celebratory at all . . . but part of celebrating is choosing your time well in order to celebrate. Imagine starting to write a book and managing your time, in the end you can publish it and it can even be a huge success, now that's something to celebrate. Hard work gives you something to celebrate. Write that song, make that Christian Tik Tok account and don't forget to have fun while you're at it.

While we're on that topic of celebrating, I want you guys to read the story 2Nd Chronicles 7:1–11 "The Dedication of the Temple." I'll only refer to the first verse since it's a long story;

> 2nd Chr 7:1–3 When Solomon finished praying, fire came down from heaven and consumed the burnt offering and the sacrifices, and the glory of the Lord filled the temple. 2 The priests could not enter the temple of the Lord because the glory of the Lord filled it. 3 When all the Israelites saw the fire coming down and the glory of the Lord above the temple, they knelt on the pavement with their faces to the ground, and

they worshiped and gave thanks to the Lord, saying,
"He is good; his love endures forever."

Everyone was worshiping, rejoicing, singing, dancing, and eating, and they were having a grand time. However, did you observe that God did not immediately respond until verse 12.

2nd Chr 7:12 the Lord appeared to him at night and said: "I have heard your prayer and have chosen this place for myself as a temple for sacrifices.

Before God had a chance to answer. These individuals banded together as one, as a nation, believing in God. While they waited, they were *worshiping*.

The important thing about this is that they never twisted celebrating in this situation, they never said, well . . . depending on how God answers, we'll celebrate, *no*. In your loneliness, in the midst of trusting God to bring you through this, trusting that He's got a plan and is about to respond. Praise Him, He will honor that. He will honor your child like faith. If your trusting God to send the right persons in your life, celebrate over what you already have, even if it's just God.

Chapter 10

What Exactly Is the Opposite of Loneliness?

What does God say the opposite of loneliness is?

✳

This is the antidote to loneliness you've been looking for. In all truth, whether it makes sense or not, the opposite of loneliness is *contentment* in Jesus Christ. It may be hard to choose between your mental health and God. I know that the lonely thoughts, feelings and urges to seclude yourself from the world almost never go away. There are times you just want to stay in your room all day without excuse. God never said that this Christian walk will be easy. The world is ruled by Satan as of right now and you serve the true and living God. Of course, he hates that and wants the absolute worst for you. Word of advice though, *always choose Jesus*. He brings contentment.

Answer this, *Is God enough for you?* I would like for you to think deeply about what I asked. If you are only content with God or if it's God *and* a job or God *and* a spouse. Then no, you have yet to learn what it is to be content with Jesus. I don't blame you, honestly, every human believes that God is a genie that answers to our every wish. When you are content with Him, when you have a relationship with Him, when you understand His characteristics and understand that He does what is best for you as His son or His daughter, you learn the true meaning of contentment. You've come to the realization that all you really need is God, and nothing is more precious than Him.

If you believe God is rejecting you or telling you that a boyfriend or girlfriend isn't a good idea or applying for this job isn't right for you right now, the truth is . . . God is telling you, "Not right now daughter." or "in the future son." because you are simply *not ready*. When you aren't ready for something and you march towards it thinking that you are, you're only causing more *mess* for yourself. It's like thinking you are ready for your biology exam without preparing beforehand. You *fail*. Now let's go back in time, to the night before this biology exam. Pretend you're in your room at 9pm, your alone but there's a reason your alone and that's to *study*. You were given that chance, the night before the exam to prep yourself, make notes and learn about the Krebs cycle. If you waste that time, you're going to *fail* the exam, but if you use that time productively you will pass. If you fail to prepare, then prepare to fail. It is the same concept with why God allows you to be lonely *first*. To prepare you for something, but you won't realize that if you're scrolling through Instagram all night, would you?

Preparing for what God has planned for you doesn't happen when you scroll through social media continuously and not spend anytime with God. So, if your asking God for something and He puts you through some secluded times without explanation, it is to prep yourself accordingly: pray, study the word and listen to when God says something to you. Keep in mind that everything God does is to protect you. He is more dedicated to you and supportive of your destiny and purpose than what you believe you deserve, as opposed to what your flesh desires.

These are some ways to remain content with the Lord:

- Let Jesus take the lead in your life.
- Serve the Lord with Thanksgiving.
- In a world full of obligation, find rest.

LET JESUS TAKE THE LEAD

As a Christian and also a pastor's kid, sometimes I sit down and I meditate over that fact that it is so easy to trust a human, for instance: a pilot to fly us anywhere in the world or a material thing like a table or chair, but it's never easy trusting God to lead our life.

> Trust in the Lord with all your heart, and do not lean on your own understanding. In all your ways acknowledge him, and he will make straight your paths. Prov 3: 5-6

It's hard to remember sometimes, but God really is good. He is kind. He is tender with His words and actions. He always loves and never rejects, He only wishes that each person repents and comes to Him, He wouldn't ever wish anyone to perish and go astray. When Jesus takes the wheel in your life, it is up to you to trust Him now. We have to familiarize ourselves with the concept that God is always looking out for us, your mental health and well-being, your joy, your peace, your so-called love-life or love-interests, your comfort, He is in deep hope that you figure out your identity in Him, the passions for your purpose which can only be revealed through Him and all of it is overseen by God. He actually cares.

We live our lives looking for them in the wrong type of people, situations, and activities. The issue is that He is the only one who understands how to get there. Allow Him to guide you. He isn't planning to take you to a certain location or frame of consciousness. He will lead you to Himself and into a greater connection with Him. In some ways, it is all about the path, since our objective is to know God personally, and as we chase Him throughout our existence, He exposes Himself to us slowly but steadily, and we sink further and more in adoration with Him.

> Hos 2:14–16 "Therefore I am now going to allure her; I will lead her into the wilderness and speak tenderly to her.15 There I will give her back her vineyards, and will make the Valley of Achor a door of hope. There she will respond, as in the days of her youth, as in

the day she came up out of Egypt. 16 "In that day,"
declares the Lord, "you will call me 'my husband';you
will no longer call me 'my master.'

We witness Hosea's unending love for Gomer in this narra-
tive; no matter what this woman did, Hosea continued to love her
and trust God. He trusted God to lead and repair their relationship
indefinitely. This book had more than one purpose: it taught us
about Hosea's terrible marriage and love life with Gomer. It's more
than just showing us how many times Hosea had to forgive her; it
also thoroughly reflects our personal relationship with God, similar to a marriage. You, believe it or not, do the same things Gomer
did, but to God. We neglect Him in pursuit of relationships,
money, fame, and success. However, in the end, God was teaching
Hosea about love, instructing him to love her even though she is
an adulteress. God was educating Hosea about Godly love.

Nonetheless, like Hosea's tale demonstrates, God decides to
ransom, or bring back, his bride—at a high price. Yet, we forget
and underappreciate this God, who's only interest is the best for
you. Let Him lead. Imagine what Hosea would've done if He didn't
know God or didn't listen to God. He'd let his lonely thoughts take
over. Allow Jesus to infiltrate your life with His plans, passions
and even His desires. Loneliness is a very distracting spirit and it
can even bring destruction, let God lead you through this. Hosea
never sat on the issue or relied on his own strengths, he let God
lead him and redeem the relationship no matter how lonely and
discouraging the situation was.

SERVE THE LORD WITH GLADNESS

Ps 100:2 Worship the Lord with gladness; come before
him with joyful songs.

Do you even realize how much easier it would be to serve God
with your whole heart and minimize the feeling of wanting company and attention? My dad once said, "An attention seeker is an
immature Christian." To be fair, every single person, somehow or

the other, craves attention sometimes. Did you know God gives you that attention? We just don't realize because we don't pay attention to God and we give Him the bare minimum.

Imagine, being carefree and content with God and His presence, knowing that in the right time, the right person and people will step into your life when He's ready for that. Remember when I said that God wants you all to Himself sometimes, well, I wasn't lying, neither was I overreacting. It's true, Jesus longs for that relationship and time with you and the reason for that is because He wants you to fall in deep love with Him first, He wants to heal the broken things inside of you because once you end up in a relationship while being broken and immature . . . that is going to be a sinking ship right there, and don't get me started on the fact that you'll be even more hurt like this.

> Isa 6:8 Then I heard the voice of the Lord saying, "Whom shall I send? And who will go for us?"

You have to be willing and obedient in order to serve God with gladness. The vision of Isaiah is a well-known Old Testament text. It is vital to remember that it all starts with Isaiah's wholehearted worship and God's purification—we must be fast to embrace God's cleaning before we can be completely equipped to fulfill His tasks, first. Once He has prepared us for His service, we must be equally ready to react with an open and willing heart when the chance arises.

> 1 Sam 12:24 But be sure to fear the Lord and serve him faithfully with all your heart; consider what great things he has done for you.

In order to serve God gladly, you have to recognize the things He does for you, no matter how big or small of a miracle it is. The prophet Samuel diligently guided the country of Israel. In his parting message, he urged the people to diligently serve God as they entered a new period of reign. They would've been reassured of God's love in their life if they kept God as their center even when confronted with a human monarch. God provides us the power to serve Him and satisfaction in doing so. Keep His promises in mind as you continue to serve Him.

I'll make this very clear, sitting on your phone chatting, watching a sermon or scrolling on Christian Tik Tok is not serving the Lord with gladness. Don't serve God halfway because you'll hate it if He treats or blesses you halfway.

IN A WORLD FULL OF OBLIGATION, FIND REST.

> Gen 2:2 By the seventh day God had finished the work he had been doing; so on the seventh day he rested from all his work.

At this horrific stage in my life, there's definitely some growing pains. Realizing I need to get my driver's license soon, everyone is treating me like a child and an adult at the same time, people's opinions and glances weigh heavily on you, and honestly, being a pastor's kid is intrinsically gut wrenching, seeing what my parents have to deal with is disturbing, and people judging the way you blink is the most infuriating thing ever. Covid did not in any way make my life any better, I felt frustrated to the point where I was moody and wanted absolutely nothing to do with anyone. As teens, I don't expect you to be "smiley" all day, it's weird feeling different emotions and even half the time you don't even know what you feel and you don't know where you currently fit in. It's either the adults or the kids and both parties aren't the best. School and my grades had taken an obsessive toll on me, I was like a busy buddy and some days I wasn't even sure if I had eaten anything because all I did was shuffle the two degrees, I had dreamed of doing my whole life. It's one thing to dream and another thing to actually get it done. All the sacrificing had my brains burning out.

Just like my world, I am pretty sure your world may be flooded with obligations too. Obligation is like a huge burden and there's no way of letting go without disappointing someone. Teens today often oppose themself as a "disappointment" or a "failure" and it's not really your fault. Some parents nowadays lack the understanding how much harder it actually is now more than ever. A survey was actually taken at my university where students were asked to say one thing, they wished they could say to their parents. Many of them implied with remarks like, "I wish you would understand how hard you push me and how hard school is." "I wish you would understand that sometimes my life is difficult, without telling me I'm privileged more than others." "I wish you knew how tired I was and I wished you'd understand." "I hope you can show some understanding when you see me napping and not tell me that I'm lazy."

Those remarks had professors shocked out of their minds and there were much more too. On that day, each lecturer was speechless saying that they were sorry to hear this then continued to tell us to keep pushing and we won't regret it. Which I think each student already knows. It's hard being in a world where you're not appreciated and you're seen as a nothing or a lazy person. It's hard being in a world doing your best and still being told you aren't good enough. This is why students and teenagers are so lonely and suffer so greatly mentally and spiritually because the burden is too heavy to hold sometimes and they've got no one to understand them.

Jesus wants to help. He wants to take the burden away. He wants to purify and regenerate your heart, mind and body. Jesus understands completely. Jesus had the pressure of literally saving the world, imagine that. That must've been so hard being humiliated on that cross, beaten and battered and then dying on that same cross just because He loved you. And even while being on the cross Jesus still lifted up every last breath, He had just to ask God to forgive us, amazing! Jesus could have backed out at any time but He prayed, He fasted, He interceded with His father continuously no matter what. He knew no one was about to understand, only God would.

When the pain and pressure start hitting deep, get deeper into prayer, my friends. Rest in God's Holy presence. There's no better place to be but in God's fiery presence. Pray, even through the lonely seasons where no one understands. Pray for the right things to come. Pray for the strength to fight through till your time on earth is done. I know how hard it is, coming from a teen herself, life couldn't get more difficult, especially while having no one to speak too on this. Jesus is here for you on that and He is more than able to pull every single one of your little hearts through this. If Jesus is named "Overcomer" and He lives in your hearts, trust me, you're going to nail loneliness to the cross!!!

www.ingramcontent.com/pod-product-compliance
Lightning Source LLC
Chambersburg PA
CBHW060402090426
42734CB00011B/2233